Supertest

Supertest

How the International Baccalaureate Can Strengthen Our Schools

Jay Mathews and Ian Hill

OPEN COURT
Chicago and La Salle, Illinois

To order books from Open Court, call toll-free 1-800-815-2280, or visit our website at www.opencourtbooks.com.

Open Court Publishing Company is a division of Carus Publishing Company.

Library of Congress Cataloging-in-Publication Data

Mathews, Jay.
   Supertest : how the International baccalaureate can strengthen our schools / Jay Mathews and Ian Hill.
      p. cm.
   Includes bibliographical references and index.
   ISBN-13: 978-0-8126-9577-9 (isbn 13 - cloth : alk. paper)
   ISBN-10: 0-8126-9577-1 (isbn 10 - cloth : alk. paper)
   1. International baccalaureate. 2. School improvement programs—Virginia—Fairfax County. 3. Mount Vernon High School (Virginia)—Examinations. I. Hill, Ian. II. Title.
   LB2351.M359 2005
   373.126'4—dc22

2005000267

Jay Mathews dedicates this book to David Weinstein,
Breigh Miller, and Lauren Reliford,
all exceptional high school students who assisted
in the research.

Ian Hill dedicates this book to IB students—
they can make a difference.

Contents

Introduction

by Jay Mathews

By then my brain was limp from too much thought, so I cannot pinpoint the moment that I realized the International Baccalaureate (IB) was worth closer attention.

I think it was near the end of the second day of the IB Twentieth-Century History examination at George Mason High School in Falls Church, Virginia. At a reckless moment, at the age of fifty-three, I had decided to take this five-hour test. As I tried to revive my depleted synapses for another round of essay questions that morning in May 1998, I heard a student announce that he wanted to leave early for a baseball game.

Erin McVadon Albright, the IB coordinator at George Mason, looked at the athlete as if he had just said Winston Churchill was a fan dancer. Her words vibrated in the small school library: "This is *more important* than baseball."

At the time I was not sure she was right, but I have come to see her point. The IB program has attracted many teenagers previously considered immune to deep thought. Historical synthesis or derivative analysis or any of a number of intellectual exercises, done the IB way, can be as compelling as a two-out triple. The program also offers a way out of an old debate about memory and insight that bedevils modern educators.

Taking the tests so many decades after my last brush with formal education was a costly stunt, I admit. Immediately afterward I had to take a long nap. But since I wrote about high school students as an education reporter, and craved the pseudo-authenticity of a few hours walking in my subjects' loosely laced sneakers, I thought it was worth the risk.

I was obsessed with challenging, high-stakes tests and how they influenced public education. Two years before I had persuaded the faculty of Mamaroneck High School in the suburbs of New York City to let me take the Advanced Placement (AP) American History test. At the last minute they pulled me out of the cafeteria test site and put me in a small room by myself, saying they didn't want to distract the real students. My theory is they feared too many sixteen-year-olds would see this balding stranger wielding a No. 2 pencil and wonder if they were doomed to remain in high school until they passed that exam.

There were good reasons for my fixation with the IB and the AP. Both tests, and the courses designed to prepare for them, expose high school students to college-level material and provide a chance for college credit. Both were created decades ago to serve tiny elites but have evolved into instruments for remaking the culture of ordinary public schools. I have seen energetic teachers use IB and AP tests to change lives. There is a remarkable power in showing an allegedly mediocre student that she can pass the same national test that the smart kids are listing on their applications to Yale and the University of Virginia.

The George Mason teachers, amused at my playing test-stressed teen, showed me why IB is even better than AP. It is available in only 450 U.S. schools, as of February 2005, but is growing fast. It has been proved to stimulate youthful interest in music and science and community service. At George Mason more than 70 percent of the juniors and seniors, an extraordinary participation rate, take at least one IB course.

Unlike most AP courses, an IB course does not allow students to skip the final exam without penalty. The AP test is usually three hours, with half of the questions multiple choice, while my IB test was five hours of essay questions. The range of IB questions reduces the student's need to cover everything at the risk of learning nothing. Depth is guaranteed by the requirement of a 2,500-word paper, which I had to defend before a panel of teachers and experts.

George Mason principal Bob Snee persuaded the IB authorities in Switzerland to allow me to participate so long as my identity was closely held. I took it as a sad indicator of the slick predictability of my paper on Sino-American relations that one faculty grader announced: "No student wrote this. It must have come off the Internet."

I learned something, however, by watching Abigail Burroughs, George Mason '98, defend her paper "The Political Implications of Leon Trotsky's Views on the New Economic Policy in the Soviet Union." Her work was deep and surprising and better than half the papers I remember from graduate school. It showed how much could be expected of young people asked to do something out of the ordinary.

In this book, I describe how this remarkably challenging and engaging program came to be, and what about it seems to work best for students, particularly American high schoolers. I chose to look at IB from the perspective of a typical public school, Mount Vernon High in Fairfax County, Virginia. I could have written about George Mason High, since the staff was so friendly and accommodating, but George Mason serves a very affluent, well-educated community, far above the national average. I wanted this book to be as relevant as possible to the majority of teachers, parents, and students involved in schools with ethnically and economically diverse enrollments.

I have woven together two stories—the birth and growth of IB in the world and the United States, and the birth and growth of IB at Mount Vernon High—to show how the ideas first conceived by a small group of educators in Switzerland eventually helped transform an American public school, one of many affected by IB. Conversations and events that I did not hear or see have been reported as the participants remembered them, with emphasis on those elements found in more than one account. In a few instances, I have identified students by only false first names. But all other names are real.

Ian Hill, the deputy director general of the International Baccalaureate Organization in Geneva, is credited as coauthor of this book because I used his extensive research on the birth and early growth of the IBO. The publisher of the book, Open Court, is owned by Blouke Carus, who once served as chair of the IB North America board and is still a member of the board of the IB Fund Inc., which works to develop outside funding for IBO projects. Some readers will wonder if these connections to the IBO make this book nothing more than a public relations exercise for IB. They are entitled to their opinions on that, but I hope they will not make up their minds until they have read the entire book. I have written every word of it and my intent is to give the deepest and most balanced description of IB possible so that parents, students, and teachers can make up their own minds about the program.

I am without question an IB partisan, although I became one when I was sweating through that test at George Mason in 1998, many years before I met, or even heard of, Ian Hill and Blouke Carus. I have been writing about American high schools for more than two decades. Based on all I have learned in that time, it is clear to me that IB and AP are the most important and beneficial improvements in American public schools in the last fifteen years. Carus obviously knew of my views before he asked me to write this book, with input from Hill's research, but I have done my best to report also what critics of IB are saying so that readers can make up their own minds.

As an American newspaper reporter for the last third of a century, I have a visceral dislike for the European spellings embedded in many IB materials, including IB's full title, the International Baccalaureate Diploma Programme. I have tried to change all such spellings to the American style, except in direct quotes of IB documents. Even then it was hard for me to put *me*'s where there should be nothing.

The book's title, *Supertest*, may inspire loathing among those who think that all tests, particularly long and important ones like the IB, are to be discouraged. To them I say, some tests are much, much better than others. Many states in the United States are struggling with new high-stakes, multiple-choice, detail-oriented tests required for high school graduation. This and the new federal No Child Left Behind test requirements have reignited the old debate between those who want students to learn facts first and then analyze them and those who want that process reversed.

Here, I think, is one possible solution: Spend a little more money for something like the IB, which simultaneously demands both memory and thought. As long as the tests are independently assessed—the IB has more than 4,500 graders in more than 70 countries—no teacher or administrator can dumb down the courses without being caught. The IB tests are designed to inspire the very best kind of teaching, without all the memorizing and drilling that troubles so many educators.

Unlike me, who slid through my two days of test questions with cute similes and glib digressions, IB students are exploring, synthesizing, theorizing, and learning how to learn. Done right, it seems to me that can be at least as important as baseball, and a model for all who want the next generation to be as prepared for the modern world as possible.

Introduction

by Ian Hill

In 1986 I was working as senior private secretary to the minister for education in the state of Tasmania, Australia. We received a request for a meeting from David Sutcliffe, who was, at the time, vice president of the International Baccalaureate Organization (IBO) Council of Foundation and head of the United World College (UWC) of the Adriatic in Italy. David was coming to Australia to promote the IBO and the UWCs in two or three of the eastern states. This was the first I had heard of the IB. It led to Australian ministers of education being represented at the annual IBO Council of Foundation meetings from 1987. I was fortunate to be that representative.

Each time I went to the council meetings in Geneva I visited a number of IB schools in Europe, including the UWC of the Adriatic, housed (in part) in a castle in Trieste, perched on a cliff overlooking the sea, right next to what was Yugoslavia. There was something special going on in these schools. The students were actually understanding (not regurgitating) and thinking analytically, creatively. There was dialogue. There was disagreement. There were other points of view. "OK, I hear what you are saying, but have you thought of. . . ." Teachers were not rewarding students with reassurance for conventional opinions. Rather, retreat from entrenched positions and careful reflection before complex issues gained respect. Global issues seemed to find their way almost effortlessly into the various subjects and made for rich discussion. Different cultural perspectives of the same historical event also led to consideration as to why people saw the event in dissimilar ways. And then there was compulsory CAS (creativity, action, service).

During my eleven years with the IBO in Geneva, I have seen many CAS projects in different countries. One of the most memorable was in Nairobi in 1995. I accompanied fifteen IB students from St. Mary's School one Saturday morning on their regular weekly visit to the pediatric cancer ward of the local hospital. Some fifteen patients, aged six to sixteen, were there. They rarely had any visitors; either their parents lived too far away or they had no parents. As the IB students walked down the rather dilapidated hospital corridor, the children in the ward spotted them and started to smile and call out greetings. Most of the children were still active and looked forward to playing games, and discussing and reading books with the IB students. Two or three of the more afflicted were not able to join in so readily. There was one girl about thirteen years old whose face was very swollen in an advanced stage of cancer. She moved around slowly or lay down.

The Dutch doctor in charge of the ward told us on arrival that one of the patients had died since the last visit. A brief ceremony was held. Astonishingly for me, there were no tears but sincere words of appreciation from each person present for the friend who had departed. They said one phrase or a couple of words each, right down to the six-year-old. It lasted no longer than five minutes. The IB students then did various activities with the children, and there was much laughter and fun. I was full of admiration for the way this African gathering made the most of their time together in the face of impending death for each of the children in the ward. There was no money for expensive chemotherapy. The IB students went out of their way to spend time with the girl who was physically most afflicted—even if it was just to hold her hand as she lay down, to talk quietly and elicit a smile from her. I followed their example and felt humble and inadequate. The doctor told me that this was the highlight of the week for the patients; there was rarely a visitor in between.

On the way back in the school bus, the students explained that their strength to undertake this weekly visit came from solidarity as IB students and the message that came through their academic experience about intercultural understanding, respect, and compassion for the human condition. Although the first couple of times had been difficult for them emotionally, they had supported each other through discussion and had come to really look forward to the hospital visits. These students had grown immeasurably as individuals. I felt privileged to be in their company.

When you do not have it, education means so much. Ask the parents I saw lined up for days in front of the Reasoma High School in Soweto, South Africa, to plead with the head of the school, already filled to capacity, to take their children. This excellent school in one of the world's most impoverished areas has been assisted by a number of IB schools in the northern hemisphere with materials and student exchange visits.

When you are afflicted with a physical disability it is just wonderful to be treated as an equal. Ask the students from the blind school who always genuinely won their weekly football match played in the dark against seeing IB students.

The IB is not just about belonging to a school; it is about belonging to a world network of like-minded people who have a common experience and the capacity to change the world for the better.

Not everyone could undertake an activity such as the one in Nairobi, but there are many other equally valid IB events—both intellectual and social—which allow students to grow in many ways.

The academic rigor of the IB is important, but its humanitarian values are everything.

A Difficult Start at Mount
Vernon High

The first year of the International Baccalaureate program at Mount Vernon High School, on a sprawling campus in the Virginia suburbs of Washington D.C., had been as bumpy as Betsy Calhoon thought it would be. Now the test scores were in and she was really in trouble.

Calhoon was a slender, soft-voiced woman with fading red hair and a deep love of teaching. She had been thrilled when her principal, Calanthia Tucker, a former college track star with a deft touch with teenagers, gave her the job of organizing the new IB program in the fall of 1993.

IB was, to Calhoon, an interdisciplinary adventure. The social studies mixed with the language arts. The math influenced the science.

But IB was also a college-level program, and it was being introduced to a public school, 1,700-student Mount Vernon High. The school was named after the famous home of the first American president located just a mile south of it on the Potomac River, but it looked nothing like that colonial mansion. MVHS resembled thousands of other suburban American schools. It had long, two-story classroom wings in the spare modern style, surrounded by parking lots and athletic fields. It also had one of the largest percentages of low-income children in Fairfax County, Virginia, and not much of a reputation for academic excellence.

"No one wanted to go to that school if they didn't have to," said the Fairfax County schools superintendent, Robert R. "Bud" Spillane.

1

So if IB was to succeed at Mount Vernon, the students were going to have to work harder than they were used to. Their initial level of achievement, even if they stuck it out, was not likely to look very impressive.

Getting more high school students to take challenging courses was very important, Calhoon thought. American public education was stalled in the early 1990s. After raising achievement levels significantly in the 1950s and 1960s, particularly for low-income and minority students, U.S. teachers had seen the scores of their students on national standardized tests flattening out. Students were graduating from high school in large numbers, but often they did not have the skills and learning to get good jobs, or survive in college. Only half of the students who started higher education ever got a bachelor's degree.

Many educators, like Calhoon, realized that much of what was being taught in high school was not very rigorous, and sometimes seemed to be little more than pedagogical pablum, a sweet, easy-to-swallow mash of light homework and short tests. The idea was to keep the students encouraged by their progress, no matter how minimal, and their parents happy with their easily obtained good grades.

Many educators thought that was a form of educational malpractice. But bringing in harder courses like IB demanded adjustments that not everyone was ready to make.

Calhoon discovered, for instance, that Mount Vernon's young physics teacher, a wonderful man who also coached the lacrosse team, did not like the IB approach to physics. It was a more experimental, hands-on course than he was accustomed to. "I don't want to do IB," he said. "I want to do regular physics." But physics, being the most difficult course taught in high school, was also one of the least popular, so there could only be one physics class at Mount Vernon. If he would not switch to IB he was going to have to leave the school. There was bitter talk about this in the faculty lounge, and the problems didn't end there.

The foreign language teachers were not happy about having to switch to the unfamiliar program. The history department was in a furor because the teachers who had agreed to do IB had their jobs protected while one of those who had asked to stick to regular social studies courses was going to have to leave because enrollment was down and the faculty had to be trimmed a bit.

Calhoon had tried her best to keep as many people as possible in tune with the benefits the new program would have for students. But at the end of that first year, she had received the big white envelope from Cardiff, Wales, and discovered that in some subjects the grades were distressingly low.

The loss of the talented physics teacher had hurt. There were seven students in the new IB physics who only got a 3 out of the possible 7 points on the exam, the equivalent of a college course C-minus. Five more students in that course scored below that, and the average score was only 3.5, below the international average of 4.39. The results in biology were not much better—an average for the school of 3.69 compared to an international average of 4.39.

And the rewards for all the Mount Vernon students' hard work seemed to be less than what had been promised. One of Calhoon's students had done particularly poorly, and this was a problem because he was the student government president, with a resume that would impress a corporate recruiter. He was the kind of student who everyone expected would go to a big-name college, and he made it clear he thought he would have gotten better grades in his courses, and looked more attractive to the Ivy League colleges he craved, if he had taken regular courses rather than IB.

But that was no longer an option for him or any other ambitious Mount Vernon student. The college admission officers, knowing that his was an IB school, would have penalized him if he had tried to avoid taking IB. That would have been to them a sign of inadequate academic strength and confidence, poison to anyone wanting to get into a brand name university.

When the student government president failed to get into the Ivy League, the effect on the morale of the IB students, and those younger students that Calhoon was trying to recruit into the program, was bad, and that was not her only concern.

Students who had completed IB soon found that their chances of getting college credit for their good work were not as great as Calhoon had hoped. Few colleges had heard of the program, and even fewer knew how to weigh it in their calculations of which high school courses approximated a college introductory course.

They knew about Advanced Placement, or AP, the much larger and more popular system of college-level exams created by the College Board. But IB was an entirely different creature, and wasn't Mount Vernon just another low-income school near a run-down commercial neighborhood? If this was a premier program, what was it doing in such a place?

Finally there was for Calhoon the disturbing realization that she was not getting nearly as many minority students into the program as she had thought she would. Barely ten percent of the first year's IB participants were Hispanic or black, and that bothered her a great deal.

Calhoon was not certain what to do about any of this. She was in her fourth decade as an educator. She had seen many teaching fads come and go. It was possible that despite her love of the IB curriculum and her conviction that she was raising her students to a new level, International Baccalaureate would become just one more experiment that didn't work out.

A Test to Unite the World

The Great War of 1914–1918, later known as World War I, demonstrated in a terrible way how distrustful and intolerant twentieth-century nations were of each other. In the uneasy peace of the 1920s and 1930s, national leaders began the first tentative steps toward global cooperation, including the establishment of the League of Nations and the International Labor Office in Geneva.

In doing that, they planted the first seed of what would become the International Baccalaureate, designed to bring nations together by broadening and deepening the way young people thought about their cultures, their histories, and themselves.

The staff for the new international organizations in Geneva came from many countries. All wanted a first-class education for their children. Their schools had to cater to a variety of languages and cultures, and at the same time prepare many of them for university education in their own countries.

A group of parents working for the League and the ILO in 1924 found two teachers at the local Rousseau Institute willing to start what became one of the great secondary schools of the world—the International School of Geneva. The first instructors were a Swiss sociologist and educator, Adolphe Ferrière, and a German scholar, Elisabeth Rotten. The school would eventually be called Ecolint, a shortened version of its French name, Ecole Internationale. At its beginning it was very small, with the first class taking its lessons in the Ferrière family's chalet.

It was the first of the international schools that would, after World War II, become much more numerous as international organizations and multinational corporations grew rapidly around the world. Ecolint would produce a steady stream of distinguished alumni, such as Indian Prime Minister Indira Gandhi, but at the beginning it fought for survival. Its first director, Swiss educator Paul Meyhoffer, complained often of the difficulty of preparing students for widely differing national university entrance exams—what the British called school-leaving exams.

In 1925 Meyhoffer sent seventeen leaders of the European educational reform movement a survey gauging their interest in a *maturité internationale*, an international school-leaving examination that would end the jumble of differently oriented courses in his school. He proposed a program of seven disciplines—history, native language, geography, biology, physics, mathematics, and a "manual occupation," which included the arts. He asked which ancient and modern languages should be included.

The reaction was not impressive. There is no record that he got any response at all. That first step toward what would become the IB got no further in the pre-World War II years. More international schools were organized to serve the children of diplomats and international businessmen, but such people did not change postings as often as they would in later years, so their children changed schools less frequently and few educators saw much need for standardizing their graduation requirements.

Some schools abroad were based on the French model and some were based on British practices, but they saw little need to cooperate. Since universities before World War II usually took all students who could afford to come, there seemed no point in having a standard exam that would distinguish the good students from the mediocre ones. The IB idea had to wait.

A High School Needing Help

Kristen J. "Kris" Amundson lived two miles from Mount Vernon High when she was appointed to the Fairfax County school board in 1991 and decided to make IB one of her first, and ultimately one of her most successful, causes. She was a writer and publicist for educational organizations in the Washington area, and had attended a conference at Princeton University in 1980 that included some chat about this new European high school program just getting a toehold in the United States.

IB appealed to her. It was a way of verifying how well a school was doing. The fact that it was European meant to her that it had high standards and a little extra prestige, what she called "plumminess"—that British upper-class thing useful in American politics. And when her school board appointment forced her to think about saving the deteriorating high schools in her southeastern corner of the county, IB immediately came to mind.

The school superintendent in Fairfax County at that time was Robert R. "Bud" Spillane, who had also heard something about IB, although the image in his mind was not too clear. He was the son of a Lowell, Massachusetts, factory worker who had been unemployed for years during the Great Depression, then managed to get a job in an aircraft assembly plant in Connecticut during World War II and start a successful restaurant after the war. His son had risen fast as a young educator, becoming an elementary school principal when he was twenty-five and a superintendent when he was thirty-one.

Results, not fancy titles, counted with Bud Spillane. He often joked that the name International Baccalaureate Programme, as it was written in European brochures, didn't look right. "Any program spelled with an extra *m* and an *e* can't be American," he said with a grin.

Spillane was a national figure in education circles by the time he came to Fairfax County at age fifty, having served as deputy commissioner of education for the state of New York and then superintendent of the Boston schools. The school board in Fairfax County, one of the largest suburban districts in the country, felt lucky to get him, even when he started to shake things up.

He opened night classes for the influx of foreign students who found it hard to juggle school and their jobs. He started the Thomas Jefferson High School for Science and Technology. And he pushed Advanced Placement very hard, arguing strenuously that it should not be just for A students, but for any teenagers who wanted to work diligently and raise their academic level.

The notion of introducing IB came gradually to Amundson and Spillane and other Fairfax educators, nurtured by their desire to raise standards for all schools and recognize the growing importance of international affairs in the Washington area. Spillane was not a patient man, and did not mind threatening sacred cows. He thought the AP program, despite its prestige, had lost its way in some schools. There were too many restrictions on who could take the courses. There were also signs, Spillane thought, of the AP teachers becoming complacent. They had the most talented students in their classes, and did not have to work very hard to prepare them for the tests.

He wanted to let the C students into AP. He had been a C student in high school. Maybe with a jolt of hard work they could catch fire as he had. Perhaps it was time for AP to have a little competition, he thought. If AP was languishing, bringing in IB might be just the thing.

His new assistant superintendent for curriculum and instruction, Nancy Sprague, knew all about IB. Her previous job had been in the tiny neighboring Falls Church, Virginia, district, where the single high school, George Mason, had IB.

Kris Amundson knew Sprague quite well, and talked to her often about what they might do for the growing immigrant pop-

ulations and declining reputations of the schools in her part of
the county. She was particularly concerned about Mount Vernon
High. It had once been the classic suburban high school, filled
with the children of middle-class military personnel and federal
office workers, as well as white-collar executives made affluent by
government contracts. Chuck Robb, future Marine officer,
future son-in-law of President Lyndon B. Johnson, future
Virginia governor and U.S. senator, had graduated from Mount
Vernon High School.

But the Route 1 corridor that plunged through that part of
Fairfax County had become a heavily commercial sector that had
many apartment complexes and cheap small houses, attracting
waves of immigrants from Latin America and Asia in the 1970s
and 1980s. Amundson, a Democrat, had been appointed to the
board as a representative of the remaining middle-class families
who remembered the old Mount Vernon High and were thinking of moving because of their doubts about the school. So she
needed to come up with a plan.

Amundson thought Mount Vernon had wonderful teachers,
and a large and spacious campus. Calanthia Tucker was a fine
principal. All it needed was a shot of adrenaline, something that
would convince the middle-class parents that there was no irre-
versible downward spiral. She had to end the embarrassment of
parents at cocktail parties who got pitying looks when they said
their kids went to Mount Vernon High.

Amundson's position on the board was not that strong at the
time. She was a member of the Democratic Party. A Republican
Party majority had captured the county board of supervisors and
was moving to appoint a majority of Republicans to the school
board. Amundson thought that would add to the traditional bias
in favor of schools in the wealthier northern section of the
county. Amundson joked with her neighbors that they were now
in the Emma Lazarus part of the county—the school system was
shipping them their tired and their poor staffers who didn't measure up at other schools, thinking that immigrant and low-
income parents in the southern part of the county wouldn't
complain.

So she launched a campaign to get IB into Mount Vernon High. She found an ally, a Republican board member named Ruth Turner, who had the same concerns about her neighborhood high school, J.E.B. Stuart. They lobbied other board members, cutting deal after deal to gather support for their pet project. Amundson went to every member of the board, asking them what they wanted in return. She told friends the other board members didn't know the difference between the IB and the NCAA, but they knew that it wasn't going to affect their constituents one way or another, and that by voting for it they could get something for themselves from Amundson and Turner.

Amundson thought she ought to have had a card printed up to remind her, whenever she voted for a new playground in somebody else's neighborhood, that it was an IB vote. By early 1993 the board had passed a budget item with money for the new program at Mount Vernon and Stuart, and Bud Spillane seemed ready to get started.

The main thing, Spillane always said, was to keep the main thing the main thing. And as far as he was concerned, the main thing was the district's academic mission. Nothing else mattered as much.

He admitted later that he did not know that the IB system virtually required that all students in the courses take the tests, unlike the more flexible AP program. He did not know that the IB tests were longer and in many ways more demanding than the AP tests. He did know that there was a controversy over whether the IB courses fit with what these students would take in college, but he had learned that the colleges could adjust. If Yale wanted to admit a bright and hard-working African American student from Mount Vernon, they would admit him and figure out his courses later.

Amundson watched with deep interest as Tucker, the Mount Vernon principal, put Betsy Calhoon in charge of the IB program. She applauded vigorously as Coleman Harris, an energetic parent who worked for the U.S. Department of Education, spent two years selling the program to the community. Both Calhoon and Harris were trusted by the parents, and all the initial signs, as far as Amundson could see, were good.

4

Getting Ready for IB

The International Baccalaureate program came as a surprise to Calanthia Tucker. She was the principal of Mount Vernon High in 1993 when Nancy Sprague, the assistant superintendent for curriculum and instruction, asked her to come to a meeting with Nancy Weisberger, the principal of J.E.B. Stuart High School.

They met in Sprague's office at Walnut Hill, a former elementary school near the Beltway that had been turned into a satellite administrative office. Sprague explained to the two principals that the board and Spillane wanted to introduce the IB to Fairfax County and thought their two schools would be the best places to start.

Sprague did not say what all three of them knew, that they had been selected because their schools, at least in relation to the other high schools in their very affluent school district, were in trouble. Their test scores were relatively low. Their middle-class parents were thinking of private school or moving to other neighborhoods. They had a higher portion of low income students—40 percent at Mount Vernon and 50 percent at Stuart—than almost all the other high schools in the district.

Sprague said they did not have to accept the IB program if they did not want it. Being a principal was hard enough without having to take on two board members' pet project. Spillane was only offering the program, not forcing it on them, and they could say no.

Both quickly said they wanted IB. In Weisberger's case, the decision was easy. Several parents in her very cosmopolitan community had been asking about IB. She knew that announcing its arrival would be a popular move. Tucker's parents and teachers were less prepared for IB, but it was an exciting, college-level program that fit what she was trying to do to improve Mount Vernon's academic reputation. She told Sprague that she also wanted IB.

Tucker had a competitive streak, evident when she was ten, running through her Chicago neighborhood as fast as an El train. In high school she was part of a youth track club. She won race after race in the 100 meter dash and had the fourth longest high jump of any high schooler in the country, over 20 feet. She was also an excellent student, so when she went to Tennessee State University on an athletic scholarship, she was not bothered by the academic load. She graduated with a degree in physical education and, with her husband, headed for the Washington area, where he had a job.

She was not very tall, only five foot six, but she had a calm certainty, a confidence in her ability to handle any situation, that children quickly sensed and respected. If anyone tried to disrupt the decorum of her classroom, they got what her daughters later called "the look," an expression that said any more activity of that sort would be deeply regretted by the recipient of Tucker's gaze.

Her first job was handling physical education at two Fairfax County elementary schools. She switched to a middle school, and then took nearly five years off to care for her small daughters. When she came back to teach middle school, the job also included science and math classes. Principals told her she had good people skills, and should consider becoming a principal herself someday. She earned a certificate in administration, spent four years as a county schools mediator resolving disputes between teachers and principals, then got an assistant principal's job. That was what she was doing when, quite suddenly, she was called to Spillane's office in September 1990.

The Mount Vernon principal had just been promoted to a central administration job, the superintendent said. Did she want to be a principal?

"So you want me to start in two weeks or so?" she said.

No, Spillane said. It was Friday. He wanted her on the job the following Monday. She took it, and found herself in a situation where her race and gender suddenly mattered in a way it had not before.

Mount Vernon High in 1990 was, for Fairfax County, a very diverse school, about 60 percent non-Hispanic white, 30 percent African American, and 10 percent other minority groups. The outgoing principal had been a white female, and the school community had very strong ideas about what they wanted to see in her replacement.

Some people called to say that she was the wrong race. "I understand you are black," one caller said.

"Yes, I am."

"We don't want you here."

Some of the African American parents made it clear that although they had no quarrel with her being black, they were upset that she was female. They needed somebody tough and male, they said, to keep their wayward teenagers on the path to graduation.

She found much more racial tension than she had expected. It wasn't a student problem. The kids were getting along fine. It was the adults. Black administrators had issues with white administrators. Male administrators were on the outs with female administrators. There had been yelling at leadership meetings, and Tucker said she was not going to have any of that.

At her first meeting with department chairs she said, "We've got leaders and some bright creative people right here and there is no reason why this school cannot move forward."

She learned about AVID, Advancement Via Individual Determination, the San Diego-based program for middle school and high school students who needed help with their study habits. She began with just one class for ninth graders. The teacher, Joyce Jones, showed them how to take notes in class, how to organize their homework, and how to budget their time. Tucker was grateful to have started that program when she was called into Sprague's office two years later and told it was time for IB.

Tucker had shared Spillane's doubts about AP. Its enrollment was low. AP Calculus or AP Chemistry might legitimately be short of qualified students, but AP English should have been welcoming every student willing to do some extra reading. She was bothered by the low number of minority students in the course.

So when IB was handed to her, she became excited. She thought it would stretch her kids. She liked its international flavor. One official at school headquarters suggested she limit IB just to students with grade point averages no lower than 3.5, a strong B-plus. But she was totally opposed to that. She had a counselor on her staff, Robert Beck, who had seen IB work wonders for all students at a State Department school in India where he once worked. When Tucker heard that Weisberger at Stuart was also in favor of open enrollment, she knew she could do the same without anyone complaining.

Betsy Calhoon, her social studies department chairman, had applied to be IB coordinator. Tucker thought there was something special about Calhoon—her drive, her dedication, and her skill at working with other teachers—so she got the job. Tucker looked for the same qualities in the other teachers she recruited for IB. She made it clear they would not be teaching just IB. She wanted them in touch with regular students, both to keep IB from becoming an elite enclave and to help them recruit more kids for IB.

It was going to be difficult to have the program ready for the fall of 1994. She and Weisberger worked together on their schools' applications and IB curricula. They met regularly after school to get ready for the visit of the IB inspection team.

There was a tricky administrative hurdle. IB required that its high schools provide five years of instruction in what it called Language B, a language other than the student's first language. It was too late to start French and Spanish courses at Whitman Middle School, so Tucker organized a summer session in foreign languages for students heading into the Mount Vernon IB program.

A spring meeting for parents and students went well. Nearly 500 people packed the school auditorium. There were explanatory brochures and veteran IB educators from George Mason High School in Falls Church to answer questions. Many parents asked how the credits earned in IB could be used in college. No one in the audience questioned the dropping of AP, a further sign that it had helped very few families at Mount Vernon.

About 100 students, rising juniors and seniors, applied. Tucker and Calhoon had found fourteen teachers ready to take on IB courses. Some non-IB teachers were worried they would have only the leftovers in their non-IB courses. But Tucker and Calhoon insisted they were also recruiting B and C students for IB.

An Idea from Geneva

The end of World War II brought the decline of the British Empire and the emergence of the United States as a world power, but that was not all that was going on. The planet was coming together in unprecedented ways. International affairs assumed an importance in business, law, and politics that they had never had before.

Many former European colonies became independent, and sought new ways of cooperating with each other, and with their former colonial masters. The nations of Europe, still traumatized by what had happened during the war, began to unite for common economic and political ends. Rapid air travel, telecommunications, the electronic computer, and the rise of information technology contributed to the development of a world that was increasingly interdependent and international. Many industrial companies took on multinational dimensions in the new political and technological climate.

The many diplomats, business executives, and technicians posted to foreign capitals needed good schools for their children. They sought instruction close enough to the style of education in their native countries to prepare their children adequately for university admission back home. But that meant a chaotic clash of different academic goals, so UNESCO convened a "Conference of Principals of International Schools" in Paris in 1949 to seek a solution.

Kees Boeke, director of the Werkplaats International Children's Community in Bilthoven, Holland, told the conference participants they needed an international diploma that countries of different languages and education systems could recognize. Alfred Roquette of Ecolint, the International School of Geneva, submitted a resolution that all schools "should experiment in 1950 with the award of an international diploma at the end of the secondary school in addition to the regular diploma." It should include, he said, proof of satisfactory knowledge of a second language and a long paper on a subject of world significance.

The minutes of subsequent international school meetings show no follow up on his proposal, but several educators and parents at Ecolint continued to promote the idea. Ecolint was the only international school that had not suspended classes during war. It took a while for it to find partners ready and willing to join it in the effort to create a new set of exams.

In 1951 parents on the Ecolint governing board joined parents involved with international schools in New York and Paris to set up the International Schools Association (ISA). They wanted parental concerns to take precedence. They were particularly worried about how best to prepare their children for college and university.

At the top of the ISA list of priorities was helping students abroad adjust to the changing admissions systems of the universities blossoming and growing all over the world. Governments had begun to realize that they had to support higher education in order to modernize their economies. This led to many more students, including those whose families had never sent anyone to college, seeking university admission with the help of new government grants. The admission process became more competitive, and created more anxiety among international school parents about the quality and relevance of the high school instruction their children were getting.

When A. D. C. (Alec) Peterson, director of the Department of Educational Studies at Oxford, first visited Ecolint in 1964, he was appalled by the Balkanized curriculum. Students who were studying physics in hopes of applying to universities in that field were divided into four small groups: one followed the syllabus for the Swiss *maturité fédérale*, one prepared for the English

General Certificate of Education A level examination, one fixed on the French *baccalauréat,* and one got ready for the American College Board Advanced Placement test.

"This was not only immensely wasteful of resources but offended against the international spirit of the school by dividing students into national groups," Peterson said in his book *Schools Across Frontiers.* "In languages there were all the problems of translation and in social studies of national bias. . . . The creation of an international baccalaureate had ceased to be solely an internationalist idea and became a practical necessity."

There were frequent suggestions that something be done about this, but it was not until Desmond Cole-Baker was appointed director of Ecolint's English-language section in 1961 that concrete steps were taken. The fact that the Geneva school was divided into a French and an English section showed what a problem Cole-Baker faced in making one exam work for all students, but he was a very forceful educator who had a missionary zeal for international learning.

Cole-Baker had seen much of the worst of World War II. He had been with the British Corps of Signals in Africa, Sri Lanka, India, and Burma. He returned to his native Ireland after the war, trained as a teacher, and then threw himself into the expansion of international education when appointed head of the science department at Ecolint in 1955. With IB, he said, he wanted to push "quarrelling humanity into the path of peace."

In 1962, shortly after Cole-Baker took his administrative post in Geneva, another of IB's founders, Bob Leach, organized a small conference that for the first time used the term "International Baccalaureate" for the unified school-leaving exam the Geneva educators were talking about. Leach was chairman of Ecolint's social studies department. He was an American Quaker who had traveled widely and had strong views about what was wrong and right with the way international students were being taught. He was also active in the International Schools Association and knew how to find money to fund new ideas.

He got a $2,500 grant for his gathering of international school social studies teachers from a UNESCO project on "The Mutual

Appreciation of Eastern and Western Cultures." Leach visited several international schools to get a sense of what they wanted to do. Throughout Europe, Asia, and Africa he found international schools in agreement that an internationally acceptable school-leaving exam was vital to their success. They also said they needed assistance with curriculum development and administration.

Leach got more small grants to study other elements of the international school curricula. In 1963 five Ecolint students took the contemporary history exam that Leach and other faculty members had written in hopes of inspiring a change to a more reflective, analytical approach from the encyclopedic fact-recall demanded by the European school-leaving exams. One of the students was accepted at Harvard, and interest in the Ecolint exam grew. In 1964 the Ecolint activists created a separate organization, called the International Schools Examination Syndicate (ISES), to turn their talk of a new testing system into reality.

For the chairman of the organization's board they chose John Goormaghtigh, an international lawyer and director of the European office of the Carnegie Endowment for International Peace. He was an Ecolint parent of Belgian descent who had been a prisoner of war in the Dachau concentration camp. He was fluent in both French and English, an important talent if he was to unite the Anglophones and Francophones behind one exam. He was at the time chairman of the Ecolint board, but he soon gave that up to devote his energies to ISES as it grew and metamorphosed into the International Baccalaureate Organization.

Still, the new group was running on thin air, its only resources being whatever free time Goormaghtigh, Cole-Baker, Leach, and the other Ecolint devotees could spare for the exam project. They operated for many years on very little money, and knew they needed more funds if they were to grow. Leach, a master grant writer, found an angel in the person of Georges Henri Martin, editor of the influential *Tribune de Genève*, one of the Swiss city's great newspapers. Even more important for the future of IB, Martin was a trustee of the Twentieth Century Fund.

Martin secured for the new organization a $75,000 grant in August 1964 to study the practicality of creating a new international exam. ISES established an office and hired former Ecolint teacher Ruth Bonner as executive secretary. Martin Mayer, author, educational consultant, and one-time trustee, was commissioned by the Twentieth Century Foundation to go to Geneva, participate in the project and write a book about it. ISES sent Ecolint teacher Eugene Wallach off on a world tour to see how this new test might be received by other international schools. In spring 1965 the ISES office moved from the prefabricated art department building at Ecolint to a neighboring villa at 12, chemin de la Chevillarde.

In keeping with the usual pattern for organizations in Geneva, the ISES planning group grew large and unwieldy, with all the clumsiness of a United Nations culture that insisted on protocol and very finely carved rules. Mayer said it reminded him of John Maynard Keynes's description of international discussions concentrating on "the determination of how many votes Brazil should have on a commission where decisions would not be taken by voting."

The core group of activists found it useful to relieve the tensions of petty diplomacy by having informal dinners at their favorite Geneva restaurant, le Rallye. Each paid his or her own bill and debated how they should apportion their favorite subjects—history, science, math, languages—into this new educational invention. Much of their conversation was also about money.

They thought there was much more to be gotten from the Ford Foundation, which was spending several million dollars on a new building for the United Nations International School (UNIS). That school planned to become the Ecolint of New York City, serving parents working for the United Nations just as Ecolint had first done for the employees of the League of Nations.

The Ford Foundation officials said they thought Ecolint's universal test idea had merit. They suggested the addition of two more members to the ISES Council to help produce a plan they could support. One was Desmond Cole, director of UNIS and no relation to Desmond Cole-Baker, and the other was Harlan (Harpo) Hanson, director of the College Board's Advanced Placement (AP) program.

Some American IB devotees were suspicious of Hanson, because they considered AP their rival for influence in American high schools. But Hanson was a witty and very persistent man, and had fought enough battles inside the College Board to dismiss with a joke or two any suggestion that he was an AP spy.

Cole and Hanson, unlike the Ecolint group, had long experience in American schools and universities and a good sense of how college entrance examinations worked in that country. Most of the IB founders saw North America as essential to the growth of the program they were about to launch. By the mid-1960s the ISES was struggling with personnel crises, questionable financial allocations, and unsatisfactory panel meetings. The presence of Hanson, Cole, and Alec Peterson, director of the department of Educational Studies at Oxford, would become crucial to getting past those problems and creating the IB.

One summer morning Cole, Hanson, and Peterson were standing outside the Café de Remor in Geneva and fretting over what to do about the Ford Foundation grant that seemed to be slipping from their grasp. Peterson recounted the conversation in his book:

"This thing will never get off the ground," said Cole, "unless someone can take it on full-time."

"I've got a sabbatical coming up," Peterson said, "and I'd do it myself, but I'm committed to teaching at Berkeley."

"I'll fix Berkeley," Hanson said, and he did exactly that. He persuaded the faculty of education at the University of California that Peterson was needed to save the fetal IB. They agreed to require just a summer of his teaching in 1967. Then Hanson and Peterson went to New York to get the Ford money.

The fact that Oxford was making IB a priority and lending Peterson to the effort was enough to get the necessary grant after just an hour of conversation with Shepard Stone, director of the foundation's international affairs program. Peterson said later he knew it was a gamble, since they had not even completed their study of the IB's feasibility. He recalled Stone saying to them as they left, "Well, boys, you're going out of here with $300,000. I wish you all the luck in the world. By God, you're going to need it."

Hanson turned to Peterson, who now had to rally the Geneva group to produce an entirely new testing system, and said with a smile, "Okay, that's that. I don't want to see you guys ever again."

Betsy Calhoon Gets Started

As Mount Vernon High struggled to establish the IB program in 1994, some teachers and parents wondered if all the turmoil was worth it. Wasn't IB just another fad that would disappear the minute the current principal or superintendent left? And wasn't it a rather elitist program, created by a lot of European diplomats for their children in fancy private schools? Was it really suited for an egalitarian country like the United States?

Calhoon listened to those concerns, but stuck to her plan. There was no one less elitist than she was. What she enjoyed most about Mount Vernon was the chance to teach an array of young people—African American, Hispanic, Asian American, Russian, Ethiopian. The school's rainbow of ethnicities exemplified life in the suburbs of the great international city, Washington D.C. Calhoon's husband Chuck was in the Marines, one of the most integrated institutions in the country. They were raising their two children, Mary Elizabeth and Thomas, to respect all races and all creeds and find a way to help people, just as their parents had done.

IB was challenging, she knew, but what was wrong with that? Some of the more affluent public high schools, including several in the wealthy northern end of Fairfax County, places like McLean High or Langley High, were loaded with AP courses. A student who took an AP course and then passed the AP test—written and scored by outside experts—impressed the admissions officers at the most prestigious colleges and had a chance to get full college credit for the work. Some of those northern Fairfax County kids were taking five or six AP courses and getting enough credit to start college as sophomores. Why shouldn't her students have a chance at that?

IB, after all, was even harder than AP, and made demands in a way Calhoon thought would prove irresistible to Mount Vernon students. An AP final exam was usually three hours long. Usually half of it was essay questions, what the College Board, creator of AP, called free response items, which were graded by human beings. But the other half was usually multiple choice questions. These were scored by machines. IB final exams were often five hours long, and had fewer multiple choice questions, often none at all.

IB tests emphasized thought and analysis, writing clearly, and making a point. Students could often choose from an assortment of questions, so that a teacher did not have to worry about covering every detail in a course, but could go deep in some areas and be assured that her students could choose those questions rather than be hung up on an issue that she had slighted in favor of going more deeply into something else.

Not only were IB final exams very long, but seniors seeking the full IB diploma had to write a 4,000-word research paper, or similar project, called an extended essay. These were graded not by the student's teacher, but by an independent reader not attached to their school. And in a few schools, like George Mason High in Falls Church, Virginia, papers in some courses were defended before a panel of experts.

It was as if the seniors of Mount Vernon, seventeen-year-olds dressed in shorts, jeans, T-shirts, and sweatshirts, had been suddenly ushered into graduate school. The emphasis was on research and depth, rather than filling in all the right boxes on an SAT or AP test. Calhoon thought her students would appreciate the difference.

Calhoon had been in Fairfax County only six years when IB arrived at her school. She was the Mount Vernon social studies department chair, a good place for a woman with a sweet temperament and a well-developed sensitivity to the stressful state of faculty relations in a large public high school.

It was at a faculty meeting that Tucker asked if anyone might be interested in serving as the coordinator for the new International Baccalaureate program that the district planned to start. She said only two of the district's twenty-three high schools, Mount Vernon and J.E.B. Stuart, would be getting IB, the first public schools in the region to have the program other than tiny, affluent George Mason High in Falls Church.

Calhoon spoke up immediately. "I would love that job," she said.

She had read about IB. What impressed her was its commitment to integrating instruction so that the language arts, science, math, and social studies teachers would all be weaving each other's lessons into their own. She had earned her master's degree in education at National University in San Diego, in a program founded on the notion that such integrated lessons were the best way to engage the attention of teenagers in a global age.

Tucker said there would be an application process for those interested in being the coordinator. But there was not much competition for such a demanding job. Calhoon was the only teacher at Mount Vernon to apply for it, and had an advantage over the other applicants who did not know the school so well.

The job would not bring her any more money. And it had, for teachers of Calhoon's dedication and quality, a significant drawback. She would have to drop all her classes in January and spend the second semester, the spring of 1994, dealing with applications and deadlines and training and schedules.

But she thought it had to be done. She understood the politics of choosing Mount Vernon and Stuart instead of the more affluent and less diverse schools elsewhere in Fairfax County. There were concerns that middle-class families might abandon the lower-achieving schools like Mount Vernon. The IB was seen as a way to give those schools some luster, and maybe even score points with those Fairfax school board members and legislators who thought the children of janitors and shop clerks and cleaning ladies could do just as well in college-level courses as the children of lawyers and doctors, if given a chance.

Calhoon had found that her students at Mount Vernon, no matter what their family backgrounds, could handle anything she gave them as long as she presented it in a way that was understandable to them. She thought IB was a fabulous opportunity to give college classes to kids who did not have many such opportunities.

Mount Vernon had only a few AP classes. There was AP Government and AP English, and that was about it. The students in those courses were usually from the more affluent homes. They were usually *not* from the many military families in the area. They were not from the many families with parents who did not attend college. No one had made much of an effort to expand the number of AP students, Calhoon thought, because there were not that many AP courses and no one was sure how difficult it would be to create more.

So Calhoon took the IB job, and held back her tears when she told her students she was going to have to leave them at midyear. She was abandoning 125 young people, 30 in her ninth-grade class and 95 in her three AP Government classes. "We have this exciting opportunity for Mount Vernon High School," she told them.

But she could not leave them with just any teacher, so she mounted a campaign to lure Bernadette Glaze away from the famous Thomas Jefferson High School for Science and Technology.

Talking to Parents

Jefferson was a magnet school in Fairfax County. It was about three miles east of Mount Vernon High, inside the Beltway, and on the other side of Interstate 395. It took students from all over Northern Virginia, but only if they had the best grades in middle school and got the top scores on a special entrance test.

Jefferson teachers, like Glaze, were also specially selected, and got a 7 percent pay raise because of the longer Jefferson school day. The school did not look very different from a typical public school. Its outer walls were weather stained and its low-slung building had a worn-out seventies look. But it was widely thought to be the best public high school in the country, with more National Merit semifinalists and AP tests than any other school. Persuading a teacher from such a school to transfer to Mount Vernon would be a singular achievement for the IB program.

Calhoun needed to get students and parents excited. The fight to change Mount Vernon seemed unique to her at the time, and exhausting. But years later, when Calhoon had become one of the most experienced IB administrators in the country, and had made several inspection trips to help other IB schools get started, she realized that what Mount Vernon went through to succeed at IB was very much what most schools went through when they decided to raise their standards significantly.

She knew many people at Mount Vernon were worried. The teachers respected Calhoun, and knew she was receptive to contrary opinions, so they asked many questions: What was this going to do to their school? Would IB add to the divisions already created by the gifted and talented and Advanced Placement programs? Was this just going to be another program that gave those same rich kids more privileges and shut out everyone else?

Calhoon plunged into a series of meetings with a steering committee set up by the district to guide the launch of IB in Fairfax County. The group included Janie Smith, who was in charge of high school curricula, Martin Abbot, the central administrator in charge of IB, and Nancy Sprague, the assistant superintendent. The Mount Vernon and Stuart high school principals, plus their guidance directors and newly appointed IB coordinators, were also on the committee. They spent long afternoon and evening hours figuring out how they were going to get this done.

The committee quickly decided this would be a program that all students would be invited to join. No one had to present proof in their transcripts that they could handle it, although the committee members did not expect to get any student volunteers who had not shown some spark of academic ability and interest.

The most daunting thing about the project was that it had to be done fast. Hiring Bernadette Glaze, called Bernie, would be an important first move. Glaze was the social studies chair at Jefferson. She and Calhoon often saw each other at the department chair meetings held once a month. Glaze was short, slender, and very energetic, with a lively classroom style that connected with modern teenagers. She also had special skills and interests that fit IB nicely. She was a devotee of critical thinking, the notion that good teaching meant encouraging students not just to memorize and understand, but challenge the material they were learning. She was very active in the Northern Virginia chapter of the National Writing Project, a group that sought to introduce intensive writing practices, including multiple drafts and frequent editing, into the American high school routine.

The English department chair at Mount Vernon knew Glaze from their Writing Project activities. Like Calhoon, he sensed Glaze was looking for a change. Jefferson was a wonderful school, but there was always the feeling that such motivated and precocious students didn't need that much instruction, and a good teacher might have more impact in a different school.

It was critical that Calhoon win the confidence of the Mount Vernon parents, and the community and business leaders who usually backed the school. This was an experiment with a foreign program that did not exactly fit the standard notion of how a high school should operate, and that was a tricky sell with American parents. Calhoon held meetings at the school for parents and students who might be interested in IB. The Parent Teacher Student Association (PTSA) president, Coleman Harris, was an energetic and vital supporter of IB. He had enormous credibility with other parents, having had three children attend Mount Vernon, including in what some parents considered the golden years when there were fewer low-income families.

Calhoon would speak at the Rotary Club one week, the Chamber of Commerce the next week. In each instance she explained that IB was something that would finally win Mount Vernon and its students and faculty the respect that their hard work had long deserved.

She spoke to students and teachers and parents at Whitman Middle School, which sent most of its graduating eighth graders to Mount Vernon. She also visited several elementary schools, where she spoke to faculty about the rising standards of the high school, as exemplified by IB, and how they might get more of their students ready for the challenge.

She thought her standard speech set the right tone: "Mount Vernon has this marvelous opportunity to become one of the few IB schools in the United States. It is an opportunity for our students to have a more global education, a more rigorous education, an education whose product will be judged by an impartial body, and we'll get to see how our kids measure up against others."

"We've always known that they were very capable," she said, "but here's an opportunity for them to prove that they are as capable as any other kids in the county and the country."

Someone in the audience would usually ask how much this was going to cost. "Well," she replied, "at this point the county will pay the annual subscription fee, which is quite expensive, about $7,000, and pay for the one-time application fee, which is $2,500. But we are going to ask families to pay for the individual exams, which will be about $45 a piece. We know many students will have trouble affording that, so we are working with the PTSA to set up a scholarship fund."

People also asked why the school was doing this. "It's an opportunity for our teachers to have access to a curriculum that is broader, that's more global," she said. "We can send teachers to training where they're going to be working with experts in the subject matter. They'll have an opportunity to network with other teachers in the same subject matter. Our kids will have a greater opportunity to be accepted at more demanding colleges." She did not tell them that some of her English teachers were also pleased by an IB reading list so exotic that it had several books that Cliffs Notes had not bothered to summarize, thus forcing students prone to take that shortcut to read the entire novel instead.

Some parents asked if students with IB diplomas would really have an advantage getting into selective colleges, given that the program was so new in the United States. "Some universities here in Virginia, including UVA, Virginia Tech, and William & Mary, are already giving kids credit for IB classes," Calhoon said. In later years she realized that was not the best argument to make for the program, for it became increasingly clear that IB's strength, just like AP's, was not in getting students credits so they could go through college faster, but in giving them the academic skills that would allow them to avoid the fate of half of college freshmen—not graduating from college at all.

When Calhoon talked to students, she realized it was better to emphasize the skills and knowledge they were to acquire in IB, rather than any college credit they might receive. "IB will develop wonderful speaking and writing skills," she told them.

"It will make you better critical thinkers. It will prepare you better for the kinds of work you will be doing in college and it will launch you into being lifelong learners."

8

Thomas Aquinas Comes to Fairfax County

Bernie Glaze was born Bernadette Maria Mulholland a few days before Thanksgiving 1946 in Philadelphia. A friend gave her the nickname at age thirteen, and although she did not like it much, it stuck. Glaze was added when she married John Glaze, a math teacher she met while teaching in the District of Columbia many years later.

Like Calhoon, Glaze was the oldest of four children. She was a good, if very shy, student at Immaculate Heart Academy in Bergen County, New Jersey. She was never confident of her school work, and her sense of what she could do suffered a jarring blow—something she never forgot as a teacher—when she turned in a creative writing assignment her sophomore year of high school.

The teacher, Mrs. Prynne, was very good at her work. Glaze would later come to admire her. But on that day, the teacher succumbed to the temptation of instructors who feel it is time to send a message to slackers.

Glaze realized that the short story she had submitted needed work. It was a silly tale about a boy and a girl missing their planned meeting on the steps of a church through some tragic mishap. But she was not prepared for what Prynne did with it. The teacher read the whole story out loud and said it was an example of how bad the writing in that class was, and how much they needed to learn. She did not reveal the name of the student, but all that mattered to Glaze was that she had been picked out as the worst writer in the class. For many years she was afraid to ever again take chances in her writing. She would remember that when she encountered students at Mount Vernon with similarly fragile egos and much less academic support at home than she had had.

She found at Immaculate Heart that she could still study and learn, even if she wasn't going to try fiction any more. The insensitive Mrs. Prynne, having given Glaze one of her worst moments, also created the opportunity for one of her best by announcing one day to her A students: "Okay, I want you to prove to the class that you're worth those As." Each was given a special assignment. Glaze was told to show the impact that Thomas Aquinas had had on the Declaration of Independence.

This was not as daunting to Glaze as it might have been to most sixteen-year-olds, because she was in a Catholic school. Thomas Aquinas was someone she had actually heard about. And she knew that one of the nuns at the school was so enraptured with the work of the thirteenth-century philosopher that she carried his *Summa Theologica* around in her pocket. Glaze politely asked to borrow it, took it home, and began to read.

She was sitting in her room on a Saturday afternoon, with the snow falling outside her window, when she looked up from the book and realized that both the Italian philosopher and his eighteenth-century American admirer, Thomas Jefferson, shared a belief in natural law. They both thought human beings were entitled to certain rights simply because they lived on the planet and were God's children. Glaze did a paper on how Jefferson's view of inalienable rights was influenced by the thoughts of Aquinas. Mrs. Prynne rewarded her with a rare compliment. "Good for you," she said.

When Glaze started college in Washington D.C. at the Catholic University of America she thought she would become a doctor, but an organic chemistry class killed that desire. What she liked about the life sciences were the patterns, the way one part of an organism influenced another, just as Aquinas changed Jefferson. Organic chemistry, by contrast, was a memorization torture chamber. It was the opposite of what she thought science should be, so she dropped it and became a history major instead.

That fed her desire to look for the connections that produced new ideas. She was assigned a paper on Lord Byron's influence on W. H. Auden. She went to the Library of Congress and requested the men's poems and a number of secondary sources. When the volumes of poetry reached her first, the thematic similarities grabbed her. She got an A on that paper, and thought about ways to make those connections even clearer, between writers, between thinkers, and between subjects.

She got a fellowship to an M.A. teaching program at Trinity College in D.C. and did a stint of student teaching with inner city kids at a summer institute. They created a model city, a way to learn about government and architecture and demographics. In 1969 she started teaching history at Spingarn High School, a predominantly African American school near the Anacostia River. There she met John Glaze, just back from the Peace Corps in Ghana, and married him in 1972.

There were problems for her at Spingarn. Many students missed class, lost textbooks, and ignored homework. But she found some students liked her lessons, in which she tried many imaginative approaches teaming with other teachers. It was going relatively well until her fourth year, when a student fondled her in the back of her classroom, and got only a reprimand from the principal. A month later, another student came into the room after school with a gun, waved it at her and said, "Get your keys and lock the door, Mrs. Glaze."

When she got near the door, she started screaming, and he ran away. She had a bruise, her blouse was torn, and she could not face coming back to the school after that, so she quit immediately. Her next teaching job, in 1974, was at Lake Braddock Secondary School in Fairfax County. She joined a team of four teachers doing an integrated course in eleventh-grade American history and literature, daily making the connections she thought were so vital.

In 1983 she began to teach Advanced Placement American History. She liked the AP course's emphasis on analysis of historical documents and its daunting three-hour final exam. Despite AP's reputation as a heavy load of memorization, she found ways to use projects, presentations, simulations, and other devices that encouraged students to connect the subject matter to their own lives.

When she taught the Revolutionary War period, she showed the film of the musical *1776* and stopped the tape after John Adams's song, "Does Anybody Hear What I Hear?" She wrote those words on the board and asked the students to write about a time when they felt that they were the only person that had a certain idea, or thought in a certain way. They wrote, and shared what they had written, then watched the rest of the film, making the connection to the uncertainties that all revolutionaries felt.

She asked the history students to write about moments in their lives when they felt rebellious. As they reviewed the relevant moments of their personal lives, she pushed them for more analysis: "So, the underlying cause of your little rebellion against your parents was. . . ." Or "What sparked that?" or "What were the symptoms of the way you felt?" She simulated the Constitutional Convention and had students play the roles of historical figures.

She was not sure she could do all that and prepare students for an AP test that included ninety minutes of multiple choice questions covering every period of American history. But, it turned out, her method worked fine once she got the pace right. The first year, scrambling to combine her method and the coverage of so much material, she only had 67 percent of students score 3s, 4s, or 5s, the equivalent of passing grades on a college exam. That was above the national average, but not good enough for Lake Braddock. Gradually she brought the passing rate up to 87 percent without, she thought, sacrificing her efforts to explore important concepts that were relevant to students' lives.

The International Experiment Begins

As the new director general of the ISES, Peterson visited Geneva frequently but worked from his office at Oxford. The first six months of 1967 he lived in Geneva while on sabbatical from Oxford, then resumed his full-time duties as head of the department of education at Oxford, with IB as his major research interest.

Long time IB activists say Peterson was a peripatetic, but extremely effective, part-time director general. Gérard Renaud looked after the Geneva office as deputy director general. After his retirement from Oxford in 1973, Peterson moved to London and worked out of what he called "a largish cupboard" at Hammersmith and West London College of Further Education. Eventually he finished out his time as director general in offices at London University's Institute of Education.

But in the mid-sixties, with the IB still an unrealized dream, Peterson and his team of advocates looked for schools that would take the program and for a group of courses that would make sense. Peterson was not happy about some of the more visionary thinking of the Ecolint teachers. In his book he quoted a 1965 Ecolint plan for a modern language program that would bring "not only an excellent command of the language, both written and oral, and a wide knowledge of the life and civilization of the language area, but also a knowledge of the literature of the language over the centuries and its place and importance in the development of world literature."

Peterson said, "As a description of a two- or three-year university course in a foreign language, it was, perhaps, not far off the mark," but "as a demand from all international baccalaureate students, including those seeking to enter the science faculties of universities, it was pure fantasy."

Peterson toured the Middle East, Africa, and South America in search of schools willing to try a somewhat more modest version of that visionary secondary school program. At a landmark 1967 conference in Sèvres, France, he announced these schools as the first IB participants: Ecolint, UNIS, Atlantic College in Wales, British Schools Montevideo, Goethe Gymnasium in Frankfurt, International School Ibadan in Nigeria, Iranzamin in Tehran, Lycée International de St Germain-en-Laye, and Santiago College in Chile.

A glance through the volumes of Peterson correspondence in the IBO Geneva archives shows how prolific he was. Peterson read and wrote French with ease. During the many times when secretarial assistance was at a minimum, he composed dozens and dozens of long, very neat, handwritten letters in English and French seeking funding, putting forward educational ideas to curriculum committees and examiners, discussing administrative and political matters concerning the ISES and IBO Council of Foundation, answering queries from schools, informing an ambassador or a minister for education of an IB project, detailing long-term plans for the future, questioning the budget figures, following up with individuals met at conferences, providing background notes for Council agenda items, and so on. In a 1968 message to Goormaghtigh, Peterson remarked as an aside, "I think I am doing about twenty letters a day." He provided the energy, the pedagogical vision, the educational stature, and the administrative competence that gave credibility to the IB at a time when it could easily have died for lack of interest.

The schools that had agreed to try IB were taking a gamble, and the gaps between the various national examination systems had not been entirely resolved. In 1965 Renaud, who had taught philosophy at Ecolint, sketched out on a conference blackboard a compromise between the two main traditions of secondary education that IB was designed to unite. Some countries, like Germany and the United States, kept their college-bound students studying a wide range of topics in the two years before they went to university. Others, like the British, had them begin to specialize. Renaud and George Bruce, an administrator of the British school-leaving exam, agreed to split the difference.

Their plan proved good enough to survive, more or less intact, into the twenty-first century. No individual subject would be required, except for mathematics and two languages. But candidates for the IB diploma would have to choose courses in at least six subjects, with math, their native language, and a second language counting as three subjects. The other subject areas would be social science (later changed to "Study of Man in Society" and then "Individuals and Societies"), laboratory science (later renamed "Experimental Sciences"), and a sixth group that became a catchall of electives, including some developed by individual schools.

Renaud also conceived the idea of a Theory of Knowledge course that all IB students would be required to take. TOK became one of the brightest jewels in the IB crown, but at its birth it was in large part a way to placate the French, who had wanted philosophy to be a separate subject area. The very first TOK syllabus can still be found in the IBO archives in Geneva, handwritten in French by Dina Dreyfus, inspector general of philosophy in the French ministry of education.

At the 1967 conference in Sèvres, UNIS principal Desmond Cole won approval for an idea that would be crucial to the success of IB programs in American public schools like Mount Vernon High. Most of the delegates from continental Europe were pushing for a system in which only students who intended to take the required six IB examinations for the IB diploma would be allowed into IB courses. But Cole, realizing that this would be a severe handicap in U.S. schools that were accustomed to students choosing individual AP courses, suggested that the six exams rule be respected, but that less ambitious students could take individual IB courses in exchange for a certificate showing successful completion of the examination in any course.

The Sèvres conference authorized the ISES to move forward on the assumption that the new testing system would continue until at least 1975, later extended to 1976. It also proposed the examination grading system—from 1 (very poor) to 7 (excellent) on exams in each subject.

The IB founders said they wanted a more qualitative, rather than quantitative, feel to the assessment. They said precise notations of performance, such as percentages, were never as exact as they seemed, particularly on essay questions, and unlikely to allow use of the extreme ends of the arithmetic scales. For instance, it was very unusual for a student to receive more than 16 out of 20 for a subject on the French *baccalauréat* exam. The most brilliant work might get a 17 but the French graders almost never gave a 20. IB examiners, on the other hand, were encouraged to use the whole range of grades and think in terms of the most brilliant work receiving a 7 and the poorest a 1. The system's designers thought this alleviated the fear of perfection that kept some examiners from giving 20 out of 20 or 100 out of 100. Giving a 7 out of 7 would not be so daunting for them, the designers thought.

At the beginning, the writing and grading of IB examinations were carried out by university experts of good standing in their own countries. This was essential, the IB founders said, to ensure acceptance by universities. As time went on, experienced IB teachers were added to the list of graders, whom IB called "readers," but even into the twenty-first century the chief examiners for each subject continued to be mostly university staff.

Educators often said they were impressed that the IB program had been drawn up by classroom teachers, such as the Ecolint team. Teachers in international schools that were contemplating adoption of IB said the Ecolint origin carried weight with them. They felt they shared with the IB founders a belief in intercultural understanding and a university education for the internationally mobile student.

In September 1967, some months after the conference at Sèvres, the council of ISES, the International Schools Examination Syndicate, decided to change its name to the International Baccalaureate Office (IBO), later to become the International Baccalaureate Organization. The council members said this reflected more accurately the purposes of the organization and avoided the term "syndicate," which had negative connotations in some countries, since it conjured up images of the mafia in the United States and crippling labor union strikes in France.

The new name created another problem, however, for which there turned out to be no quick solution. The term "baccalaureate" was confusing to many people who heard it, particularly in the United States. The Europeans had pushed down into their equivalent of high school many courses that would be considered college courses in the United States, the sort of courses that led to a bachelor's (baccalaureate) degree. Peterson remembered being warned that the new organization might even be sued for false pretenses in North America for using the term "baccalaureate" for high school courses, when it really meant higher education. But if AP courses were winning college credit for high school students, the IB founders thought they might be able to get the same kind of recognition.

The IBO formally declared that its mission was to create and administer the examination that had been agreed to at the General IB Conference in Sèvres. Three years later IBO was affiliated with UNESCO as a non-governmental organization (NGO).

By 1970, after two years of trials, the first twenty-nine students used IB examination results to enter universities. The experiment was underway.

Welcome to Mount Vernon

For eight years, Bernie Glaze had enjoyed teaching history to the young prodigies of Thomas Jefferson High, and when the Mount Vernon English department chair suggested a transfer, it seemed like an unlikely move.

She was being asked to leave Jefferson, probably the best high school in America, and she would lose the 7 percent pay bonus. It didn't seem fair that teachers at Mount Vernon, where the students were often harder to reach, earned less that the teachers at Jefferson, with the most teachable students anywhere, but that was the way it was, and leaving Jefferson, for most teachers, did not have much appeal. Her husband was still a math teacher at Wilson High School in the D.C. school system and it was all they could do to scrape together the $30,000 a year they were paying for their son Chris's first year at the University of Chicago.

Glaze visited Mount Vernon to observe an AP Government class. The class sizes were too big, she thought. She didn't like the school's schedule. She was not a morning person. She would have to show up at 7:00 a.m. at Mount Vernon, whereas at Jefferson she did not have to drag herself to work until 8:00 a.m.

But there was something about IB that intrigued her. One of her friends when she was in graduate school at Trinity had been Barbara Walker, one of the first teachers at the Washington International School (WIS), a private school that was one of the first places in the United States to embrace IB. Glaze remembered the new WIS building that Walker showed her, and Walker's excitement at being part of one of the most sophisticated and integrated lesson plans ever invented for high schools.

Walker said IB was dedicated to showing American teenagers how they could be both challenged and excited about what they were learning.

Back then, Glaze wasn't sure she was smart enough to teach at a school like that, and perhaps she still wasn't. She took a negative tone with the Mount Vernon English department chair, but he asked her to think about it, so she did. She had had eight years at Jefferson, a good run. And there had been some recent annoyances. The Jefferson principal had changed the administrative system and she was no longer a department chair. It had been done in an abrupt way, and she was not feeling good about it.

It was Christmas time, a season for unexpected happenings. She had a peculiar dream. She was at Mount Vernon High, teaching kids who were not quite as precocious as the students at Jefferson, but they needed her. She woke up and said to her husband, "You know, I think I am going to go there after all."

The Jefferson principal called her in when he heard the news. "So you're going to do this?" he said.

"Yeah, I think I am."

"So you're going back to a real school?"

"Yeah, I think I am."

She let Calhoon know right after Christmas. She wanted to start reading about IB, but there wasn't much time. She had to transfer to Mount Vernon almost immediately, and that was just the first of the new things she had to tackle.

It was fun working with Calhoon. They were both Irish American girls from big families, first borns with good marriages and instincts for trying something new in their classes. But after all those years at Jefferson, Glaze had lost touch with the atmosphere of a normal public high school in the 1990s. Mount Vernon had teachers and administrators with walkie-talkies, ready for trouble. There were a few fights, many more near fights, and the county police officer assigned to Mount Vernon had a Wall of Shame in his office with the student identification cards of all the kids who had been kicked out of school.

Mount Vernon had some great teachers, but there were also some who responded to students who needed help with nothing but more rules and more worksheets. Glaze was going to be teaching Calhoon's three AP Government classes, almost 100 students in all, as well as running the social studies department, and she was a stranger to most of the teachers she would be working with.

She felt lonely, getting into her old blue Honda Accord each morning and making the drive from Capital Hill where she lived, down through Anacostia to the Beltway and over the Potomac River via the Woodrow Wilson Bridge to Route 1 and south to Mount Vernon. The kids in her AP classes, still resentful of Calhoon leaving them, had not welcomed her warmly, and she wondered if she had made the right decision.

Calanthia Tucker sensed her mood. The principal caught up with Glaze late one afternoon as she was heading to her car, her arms loaded with essays she had to correct. Tucker stopped in front of the new teacher, looked at her sympathetically and with her best smile said, "Bernie, I want you to know how blessed we are to have you here."

Glaze thanked her, put the papers in her trunk, sat down in the driver's seat and before she turned on the engine, burst into tears. She felt better. She said to herself, "This whole thing is going to be okay."

Three Big IB Ideas

The IBO's first office, in a villa across Lake Geneva from the UN building, would plant itself in the memory of IB staffers. According to Gérard Renaud, it was owned by a married couple named Dawint, but Mr. Dawint lived in another part of Geneva and came to lunch with his wife just once a week. Mrs. Dawint, an artist, lived downstairs with her many paintings. The IBO office was upstairs, with a separate entrance from the outside.

IBO staffers found the neighborhood of Cologny to be quite pleasant. For a few months in 1967, Peterson lived in a house just 200 meters from the villa. He spent many evenings in the local bars, meeting the locals and brushing up his spoken French.

One wing of the IBO office was dubbed the Galerie des Glaces in honor of the famous and colorful gallery of the same name in the Palace of Versailles. The IB diploma examination timetable was put together in that room by writing down the tests for which students had registered on little pieces of cardboard in different colors to represent the different subjects. The schedulers put the colored cardboard indicators on the floor of the Galerie des Glaces in their proper order to make sure they were not asking students to sit for different examinations at the same time.

The most vivid account of life in the office was published in the May 1970 issue of the IBO's semiannual bulletin, in an article entitled "A Fly on the Office Wallpaper." No human writer took credit for it. It was composed from the point of view of an insect that had flown in through a window at a busy time.

"It is an odd place indeed," the author wrote. "It is a most beautiful apartment, with all the grace and elegance of bygone centuries, but surely I can see telephones, tape recorders, typewriters (electric, of course), an accounting machine, a very modern copying machine, which hardly ever stops buzzing and clanking, and many other signs which point to the last quarter of the twentieth century. The long table under the glittering chandelier gives promise of gracious glass and silver, good food and wine, the bare shoulders of beautiful ladies, and the chatter of the gossip of cosmopolitan Switzerland. But no, the table is covered with examination papers and envelopes, and the only (fairly) bare things in sight are the minied legs of the young secretaries."

He described the view from the office windows, "the rippling water of Lac Léman, and behind are the snow-covered Juras," as well as "primroses and daffodils in the garden" and "pigeons, tits, robins" and many other birds. He said it was a very quiet neighborhood with few buses, no trains, and just an occasional roar of a jetliner taking off from the Cointrin airport across the lake.

It was, he said, the season of the first real IB, with the examination ready to be sent to the schools that would administer them. The office was filled with strange words like UNIS and Ecolint and Ibadan and Iranzamin, as well as Alpha syllabus, Session B, Rank-Xerox and cassette-recorded oral.

The fly captured some of the spirit of the IBO in its early years. From the beginning the teachers who designed the program prided themselves on making do with what they had. Peterson told the story of Philip Heafford, a specialist in physics education at Oxford, who had to get to a meeting of other IB physics teachers in Sèvres, but was stymied by a series of strikes at French airports and seaports. He was a persistent person, both as a physicist and in his leisure hours as a mountain climber, and so he went to Dover, bought a bottle of brandy, and walked along the quay to see if he could use it to persuade a visiting French fishing boat to take him across the Channel.

"Can you give me a lift to Calais?" he shouted to one fisherman.

"Only if you're a mountaineer, Monsieur."

"Why that?"

"I can't take you into Calais. But I could land you on the rocks at the base of the light-house, if you can manage the climb."

He could, and got to his meeting in time. Resourcefulness was part of the IB culture, as was a fondness for new ideas that would help educators struggling with an increasingly complicated world.

In 1970 the IBO published the first *General Guide to the International Baccalaureate*, in English and French. It contained rules, instructions, university recognition agreements, and subject programs for the examinations of 1971, 1972, and 1973. It offered what was a very innovative approach to secondary education. It insisted on a broad range of assessment tools, including course work, written examinations, oral examinations, and practical assessments. The idea was to move away from regurgitated knowledge to a more critical, personal approach.

The guide said: "All forms of assessment attempt to bring out not the candidate's ability to memorize, but the extent to which he has assimilated and made his own the subject in which he is being tested."

IB curriculum and examinations showed the influence of three countries. The British brought the essay-type questions. Multiple choice and short answers came from the United States. The French contributed in-depth textual analysis and oral examinations. But the IB program was not based on the most frequently occurring common aspects of pre-university courses in these nations, for those developing the IB exams were often those most dissatisfied with their national systems. The opportunity to exchange ideas across national frontiers and change the way things were done in their own countries was one of the reasons why they had joined IB in the first place.

The founders thought they knew how to deepen and broaden the typical academic load of a student in his or her mid-teens in the Western world and its cultural offshoots. There was, they thought, too much the feeling of a forced march toward university life. Students focused on getting good grades, and good scores on their national exams, so that they could get into the colleges they wanted. It was hard in that atmosphere to experience the thrill of exploring the unknown. The founders wanted IB students to feel like Lewis and Clark mapping the unexplored Louisiana Territory with eyes open to all possibilities, and not feel so much like cyclists pedaling frantically to beat all their competitors in the Tour de France, without any time to stop and appreciate what they were seeing.

Their effort to alter the course of university preparation led to three great IB innovations that distinguish it today from other college level programs, such as AP. Each of the ideas grew from the IB founders' notion of what an educated person ought to be, and became the parts of the program that students praise most often—the extended essay; the creative, aethestic, or social service activity (CASS); and the Theory of Knowledge course (TOK).

The extended essay had many influences, but one of the most important was Kurt Hahn. He was a prominent German educator who escaped a Nazi jail before World War II through the intervention of British Prime Minister Ramsay Macdonald and resumed his career in Britain, where he had a deep influence on several of the IB founders, particularly Alec Peterson. Hahn said high school students needed an intellectual outlet for what he called their "grand passion." That led to the requirement that every candidate for the IB diploma conduct a significant piece of research on a topic of his or her own choice.

The extended essay was first introduced as something called "independent work," required as part of the course in the student's first language, and then in other subjects. The idea was to develop research skills and encourage the kind of critical thinking learned in Theory of Knowledge. This produced a heavier workload than was intended, and led to a proviso in the 1972 IB guide that if a candidate was taking three higher level courses, each requiring an extended essay, the student would, "with the agreement of the examiner concerned, be permitted to forego the extended essay in one of the three subjects."

In 1974 this load was lightened further. Students were required to submit "one extended essay or project work" in one of the six subjects, which would be marked by the teacher, reviewed by an external examiner, and "if necessary, the work would be tested further by the cassette oral method," in which the examiner sent a list of questions to the student who was required to respond orally on the cassette.

The extended essay had to apply to one of the six IB subject areas and be about 4,000 words in length—the equivalent of about sixteen typed, double-spaced pages. It had to be done over four to six months of the candidate's own time under the guidance of a teacher, and be graded by an outside examiner.

A required paper of this length, to be graded by someone who did not work at the student's school, was almost unheard of in American public high schools and was not that common in the rest of the world either. IB educators wondered how it would be received once the program spread beyond the first few student participants, whom everyone assumed would be unusually brave and talented. IBO officials were pleasantly surprised when examiners and teachers began to report that the extended essay was in many students' minds the highlight of their two years in IB.

Peterson said he was stunned at how much energy students devoted to their own versions of Hahn's grand passion. "We very soon found that we had to put back the date of submission of the extended essay to some months before the completion of the course," he said, "because schools complained that too many students were becoming so deeply involved in their extended essay topic that they were neglecting the rest of the course and might fail their diploma examinations."

The second new idea, the creative, aesthetic, or social service activity, was also inspired in part by Hahn, who had called for a social service dimension to high school learning. Hahn was to gain fame as the father of the Outward Bound movement, a way to forge character by taking students into the wilderness, and this part of IB had the same roots. Peterson was particularly pleased with this aspect of IB, for he did not like what the competition for good college spaces was doing to young people's choices of how to spend their spare time. In *Schools Across Frontiers* he recalled a conversation he had with an ambitious student early in his career when he was the headmaster of Dover College, a British secondary school.

"I'm afraid I shall have to give up playing in the orchestra next year, sir," the boy said to him.

"But why? You're our best violinist and you love it."

The student was applying to Bristol University, which had many stringent requirements for getting into its chemistry program. "I can't spare the time," he said.

The IB founders realized it would be far too difficult, given the different circumstances in each IB school, to prescribe a certain kind of significant activity outside the classroom. The first proposal, in 1968, was for a compulsory course "of theoretical and practical initiation into the Fine Arts" for the equivalent of one afternoon per week. In 1970 "physical and social service activities" were added to the requirement, with a teacher comment on the performance on all three to be part of the regular assessment.

The idea was to encourage active involvement in the aesthetic (the arts), the physical (sport or exercise), and the social (service inside and outside the school) and contribute to the growth of the whole person rather than just academic development. Such a requirement was part of Atlantic College, the internationally oriented school Peterson and his patron and wartime commander, Lord Mountbatten, had helped start.

So every IB student set aside the equivalent of one half-day a week for engagement in some sort of creative, aesthetic, or active social service activity, the CASS requirement. Many schools went beyond that basic commitment. The amount of performing, interning, creating, and serving done by IB candidates became a distinguishing mark of the program.

In 1989 CASS became CAS, for creativity, action, service. "Action" meant physical exertion in sport, expeditions, mountain climbing, gymnastics, and other strenuous activities, something that had not been part of the earlier title. Community service was encouraged, but the IB administrators realized that in some cultures and geographical locations this was not easy to accomplish, so the single word "service" was said to include service to the school itself, such as assisting with younger children, organizing clubs, or launching environmental awareness activities. "Creativity" retained the connotations it had had from the beginning.

Many of the CAS projects around the world came to be linked with IB's emphasis on intercultural understanding. IB students worked with refugee families to reinforce the language of the host country and provide support. IB schools assisted local schools in the developing world with books, materials, and lessons. One IB school in Uganda provided moral support to the families of HIV-positive parents by recording their oral histories.

The third big IB idea, the Theory of Knowledge course, grew from Renaud's deal with the philosophy-conscious French, but became more important through the work of IB's first examiner for TOK, Dina Dreyfus.

She worked for the French government as an inspector of philosophy programs. She was an imposing figure among French intellectuals, and was married at the time to Claude Lévi-Strauss, the world-renowned anthropologist. She was surprised when Renaud told her some people thought she was arrogant. She tended, as he did, to get lost in her work. One day they worked so late on the IB philosophy exam that the caretaker mistakenly locked them into the villa, forcing Madame Dreyfus to climb through a window and jump out onto the lawn.

Years later many American students and teachers would look at Theory of Knowledge as a welcome expansion of the brief and frequently misleading units on philosophy that would often be no more than a few days wedged into a high school history or civics course. But TOK was initially designed to address a complaint the IB founders had about European schools that was not entirely unfamiliar to Americans.

Peterson said there were two glaring weaknesses in the structure of European instruction. "The first was the tendency which most students had to study their different subjects in watertight compartments," he said. "Not only did they fail to relate apparently disparate subjects such as physics and history to each other; they often did not seem to see connections between literature and psychology or history and literature. Their teachers often did not seem to have the time to help them to see such connections, possibly because the form of the examinations positively discouraged it.

"The second weakness was the failure to make explicit in the minds of students the differing forms which academic learning and knowledge take," he said. "The intention of the course was to help the student to think about the questions which underlie the nature of knowledge as presented in the school disciplines and in his daily life."

So the General Guide to the International Baccalaureate for the Theory of Knowledge course broke it down into several parts:

1. Language and logic
2. Scientific activity and the formation of scientific concepts
3. Mathematics and reality
4. The constitution of a human science
5. Historical knowledge
6. The nature and basis of moral and political judgment
7. The nature and basis of aesthetic judgment
8. Opinion, faith, knowledge, truth

There was one other part of the IB plan that required extended discussion before it could finally jell. This was the sixth course, the last side of the hexagon that became the IB symbol. When the first exams were designed in 1968, students had a choice for what to do as their sixth course: an arts subject; a third language, either classical or modern; a second subject from the "Study of Man" or experimental sciences list; or a new course designed by the school and approved by the IBO.

This gave IB teachers an outlet for their creative juices, and many of them responded enthusiastically. By 1973, eleven school-based subjects had been developed and accepted: drama, filmmaking, contemporary music, Middle East societies, comparative regional studies, political theory, the UN and disarmament/aggression, environmental studies, marine studies, photographic science, and astronomy.

Each new course was graded by the teachers at that school, with an IBO examiner stopping by to check. The course syllabi were distributed by IBO to any other schools that wanted to look at them, and some were later adopted as full-fledged diploma subjects, such as music in 1979, environmental systems in 1989, and theater arts in 1996. Film became the first school-based subject to be approved as a part of the diploma program in the twenty-first century.

By the 2000s there were more than two dozen school-based courses, including accounting; agricultural science; ancient Greek civilization; ancient history; art history; Asian arts; beginners' Nynorsk (one of Norway's two official languages); Brazilian studies; Chile and Pacific basin studies; Chinese studies; Classical Greek and Roman studies; electronic music; electronics; European studies; Fijian studies; historical and contemporary Brazilian studies; nutritional science; peace and conflict studies; political thought; science, technology, and society; social studies; Turkish social studies; United States history; world cultures; world politics and international relations; and world religions.

Each school-based course is a Standard Level IB offering, lasting at least a year. The IBO requires that each has sufficient academic rigor, fits IBO objectives, and is conducive to the kind of final examination that is typical of Standard Level courses. Enrollment worldwide in the school-based courses is much smaller than in full-fledged IB courses, in part because there is less certainty that colleges will accept them for credit.

Peterson thought this approach would be an ideal way to adjust IB to what he called "the needs of the whole person." His idea was to develop Standard Level subjects that were not necessarily needed for further study, but would conclude with diploma examinations and take the school-based subjects as a model. Three interdisciplinary programs being pioneered by the IBO—a literature and arts combination called Text and Performance, a humanities and sciences combination called Ecosystems and Societies, and a humanities and arts combination called World Cultures—are designed to fulfill this vision.

Training in New York

Once Glaze arrived at Mount Vernon High in February of 1994, she faced a huge task. Not only was she taking over Calhoon's classes, but also she had to create an entire social studies curriculum for the first year of IB just six months away.

The guidelines that IB had provided for history included pages and pages of study topics. Glaze wondered how she and the other teachers in her department were going to cover all that. That was, of course, her American way of looking at the task. IB wanted something different. There might be many topics on the IB history exams, but students could choose from many essay questions. IB was encouraging American schools to use the topics as just a framework. Each school and each teacher could decide what was best to concentrate on.

This went to the heart of a long, bitter debate among American educators, which became more divisive as standardized tests were adopted as an important way of rating U.S. schools in the 1990s and 2000s.

The new state tests used to determine which schools would be rated "needs improvement" under the federal No Child Left Behind law, as well as the SAT II and AP tests used to determine how well-prepared students were in certain subjects, demanded that teachers cover a certain amount of material. Since, for instance, an AP U.S. History teacher could not predict if there would be any questions on the Missouri Compromise or the Spanish American War or the Gadsden Purchase, that teacher had to cover all those topics to prepare her students for the test. Half of each AP test included some essay questions that would allow students limited choice of subject, but the other half of the AP were multiple-choice questions that might cover anything.

Some American teachers, inspired by the writings of educational psychologist John Dewey and modern day Dewey disciplines such as Theodore Sizer and Deborah Meier, said trying to cover everything was a recipe for frustration and once-over-lightly teaching. They wanted teachers to pick a few topics in history, or whatever else they were teaching, and go in deep. For instance, in teaching the writing of the U.S. Constitution, many teachers had found that if they took two weeks to organize a simulated Constitutional Convention, with students playing the roles of James Madison, Alexander Hamilton, and the other founding fathers, that part of American history came alive and remained with them for the rest of their lives.

But educators who wanted students to master all the main points of the American story said that although they admired and approved of such exercises, if taken too far they could result in what they called hobby teaching. They said teachers should not be allowed to indulge their personal interests and avoid addressing those parts of the historical record that did not interest them. It was such dallying that led many high school students to never get a lesson on anything that happened after World War II. The typical American history class always ran out of class time by 1945.

The IB history tests were a godsend to teachers like Glaze, who rooted for the Dewey-Sizer-Meier side of the argument. Sizer's famous slogan was "less is more." The IB exams, although as many as five hours long in total for one subject, allowed students to write deeply on just a few selected topics. On the IB Higher Level Twentieth-Century History test, for instance, the first two parts covered twentieth-century issues, with some choices, then the third part offered twenty-five questions, of which the student only had to answer three based on the region his or her class had chosen to study in more depth.

Glaze planned to cover the topics she was teaching with the completeness that her students deserved, but under the IB system she could spend more time on some subjects and experiment with projects and presentations and other ways to engage teenagers' interest. If she wanted to devote extra time to those periods in which she had read most extensively, like the awakening of social activism in the late nineteenth century, she could do so without worrying that her students would not get enough information on the Civil War to answer a range of multiple choice questions. Unlike the AP exam, the IB history exams had no multiple-choice questions.

The two IB social studies courses Calhoon and Glaze decided would work best at Mount Vernon were History of the Americas, which would be their regional study, and Twentieth-Century History. They fit the state and county requirements for history instruction, and would be taught as two-year courses, what IB called its Higher Level, or HL, courses. But there were also Standard Level, or SL, courses in anthropology, philosophy, economics, psychology, and geography that could be completed in one year. Glaze decided she wanted to teach History of the Americas.

At the July training session at the UN International School in New York, Glaze stayed in a fashionable little hotel in Chelsea. She liked UNIS, but was not entirely pleased with the IB training course. For a program that encouraged students to learn by exploring topics on their own and making unexpected connections, the IB sessions were annoyingly traditional—the Mount Vernon teachers taking notes while the IB trainers lectured.

She thought this might have been the result of picking trainers based on how well their students scored on the IB tests. That certainly made sense, she acknowledged, but high scores were still going to be a function of family income, as they always were. She thought her task at Mount Vernon was to find a way to bring the excitement of an international learning program to students who did not have much money and thus rarely left their neighborhoods. That was going to take more than just standing in front of the class, as the IB trainers were, and telling students everything she knew. But she did not want to embarrass Calhoon and Tucker, who had been kind enough to send her on an all-expenses-paid trip to New York, so she took many notes and politely kept her mouth shut.

When she returned to Mount Vernon, she found the summer days dwindling and the launching day for IB approaching. She had teamed with Mark Rogers, who was going to teach IB History of the Americas at J.E.B. Stuart High, the other Fairfax County school starting IB. Rogers also attended the New York training sessions, but he and Glaze knew that they were going to need more help, and so they tried to assist each other as much as they could.

They sat down at Rogers's new dining room table in his apartment in Old Town Alexandria, near the Wilson Bridge that was Glaze's route across the Potomac each day. They surrounded themselves with textbooks and other reference materials. They had a good sense of the material, but how to teach it was another matter, and they tried ideas out on each other as the big day drew near.

The First IB Exams

The IB founders had worked out the general approach they wished to follow in their examinations, but they still had to write the questions—and keep their promise to measure what their students had learned as well as encourage deep teaching.

There were many models to choose from. The British method in English exams was to ask for many short essays in response to fairly specific questions, such as, "Milton's Satan moves us because he is able to convey dramatically what goodness is. Discuss." The students were required to answer all of the questions, giving a sense of not only the quality of their analysis but whether they had read a representative slice of the required books. The French and German method was quite different for literature exams. They might ask for one long composition or critical analysis of a poem the student had not seen before, and allow four or five hours to write the paper. The American system, at least for college-level examinations, was somewhere in the middle. The AP exams included some multiple-choice questions, and were closer to the British than the continental European model.

Requiring several short essay questions, as the British did, produced a more reliable measure of competence than the deeper and narrower French and German approach, psychometricians said. Their research showed that the wider the range of questions asked, the more confidence the examiners could have in knowing the examinees knew the subject matter.

But the IB founders were determined to emphasize the depth of thought and learning in their classes. Peterson in particular, as a leading British expert on the educational methods of his own country, saw what kind of teaching and exam-taking that system had produced, and he thought that it was not in keeping with what he and the other IB pioneers had promised to do.

"If . . . the objectives of the course were conceived as the awakening of a life-long interest in and critical reading of good literature, the development of a precise and personal style of expression, and the maturing and refinement of the moral and aesthetic judgment," Peterson said in his book,

> the question immediately arose whether a method of assessment which relied so much upon testing recall was really valid. It was argued that, faced with questions of such complexity and so little time in which to answer them, the average candidate could not possibly write anything valuable which he originally felt or thought at that moment, but was forced into reproducing his previous thoughts or, even worse, the thoughts from a textbook or a teacher transmitted in note form, and that this explained why English examiners so regularly complained that the candidates answered, not the question asked, but the nearest equivalent to which they had already memorized an answer.

Peterson called this the "backwash" effect. If the examination required a great deal of quick recall of specific texts, then the teachers would require a lot of memorization in their classes. If the examination demanded longer, more thoughtful essays, then that is what the teacher would have students practice during the year.

The IB founders decided the way to make sure that students were not improvising based on very little reading was to include, at least in the Language A exams that tested students' understanding of their first language, an oral examination. IB examiners, who were often teachers at neighboring IB schools, could sit down with each candidate and ask enough specific questions in a relatively short time to separate the serious students from the clever slackers.

Peterson loved to participate in oral exams when he visited IB schools, because he saw this thesis proved repeatedly. A thirty-minute interview with two candidates in New York convinced him that one of them had not read *The Mayor of Casterbridge* and that the other had been so excited by *The Waste Land* that she had taken the trouble to read Jessie L. Weston, the English folklorist whose writings on Arthurian legends had influenced T. S. Eliot as he wrote his famous poem.

But the oral examination system had its drawbacks. It was expensive to pay examiners to travel to other schools, even if it was just a day trip in an automobile. The reliability of the examiners could not always be counted on, since they were often friends of the IB coordinators of the schools they visited and may have taught at those schools themselves in previous years. The founders continued to search for ways to ensure that the results of these examinations were a valid measure of what the candidate knew.

The American fondness—and the contrary European loathing—for multiple-choice questions became a lively issue as the IB exam writers tried to enhance the reliability of what they were doing. A few of the exams, such as the Language B test for candidates studying a second language, did use multiple-choice questions to get a sense of weak spots in students' comprehension of the language. Critics of multiple choice said this was an unnecessary crutch. They pointed out that because the IB did not have the money or the sampling size to test each question in a professional way, there would always be some clumsy questions that would embarrass the IBO.

When this came up at an IB meeting, Peterson recalled, Harvard professor Fletcher Watson broke down the problem into its parts: "Let me see. This suspect item is one of forty in the Language B examination. What weight within the Language B examination does the multiple choice section carry?"

"One fifth of the total marks."

"And Language B is one of the six subjects, graded on a 1 to 7 scale which make up the IB diploma total?"

"Yes."

"Then we are talking about one-fortieth of one-fifth of one-sixth of the candidate's total assessment. Gentlemen, I don't think you should worry too much about it."

While the debate over the precise form of the exams went on, the IBO office continued to move from one place to another, trying to keep its rental expenses as low as possible in high-priced Geneva while adjusting to rapid growth in its activities. It was housed at chemin de la Chevillarde, adjacent to Ecolint, until October 1967 when it moved to the charming villa at 37 route de la Capite, Cologny, described by the literate fly in the IBO newsletter. In August 1970 it moved to larger premises at 12 chemin Rieu, Florissant, owned by Union Carbide.

As the organization expanded, that building also proved too small and IBO moved to 1 rue Albert-Gos, still in Champel. In December 1974, thanks to an offer from the Canton of Geneva, the office moved to the other side of the Lac Léman and into the Palais Wilson, 52 rue des Paquis, where UNESCO's International Bureau of Education and the International Schools Association were already located. The building had housed the League of Nations and was named after the League's initiator, President Woodrow Wilson. In December 1983, still growing, IBO moved again to 15 Route des Morillons, Grand-Saconnex, near the World Health Organization and the International Labor Office, where it remains today.

IB's survival depended on the strength and persistence of its growth. That meant persuading more high schools to use the exam and more colleges to welcome applicants who had earned IB diplomas. Two key first users, Atlantic College and UNIS, had their doubts about the trial examinations in 1969, but agreed to participate in the 1970 test administration, the first to be used in college admission and placement. There were only twenty-nine diploma candidates that year, but an upward trend took hold in subsequent years.

Universities around the world turned out to be not nearly as resistant to welcoming the IB students as some of the founders had feared. The rising numbers of families living abroad and seeking higher education outside their home countries had

Year	certificate candidates	full-diploma candidates	diploma pass rate 4s and above
1970	206	29	69%
1971	525	76	70%
1972	480	151	63%
1973	529	311	76%
1974	288	386	80%
1975	354	377	75%
1976	433	567	76%

flooded university admissions and placement offices with more school-leaving exam results than ever before, and the differences between them were confusing. It made sense to many universities to cooperate with an international, foundation-supported experiment that might give them a common international standard on which to judge such applicants.

The IB results, after all, were rarely the key determinant of admission. Universities placed much greater weight on school grades, activities, and teacher recommendations. In American universities, where the greatest number of IB students sought admission, entrance decisions were made in April, before the IB students took the final senior year examinations that would determine if they earned an IB diploma or not. The IB results became important, however, in deciding which introductory college courses they might skip once they were admitted.

Harpo Hanson, who had helped secure the Ford grant, was well known to the admissions deans of many of the most selective American colleges because of his position as head of the College Board's AP program. It seemed odd to some of the admissions officers that Hanson was also working for what looked to them like one of his competitors, but he devoted himself to winning acceptance for the IB program. He told confused admissions officers that he did not see IB as competition for AP, but as a way to expand choices for both students and universities.

Harvard and then Princeton agreed to offer sophomore standing to students who had earned an IB diploma, although few students used their credits in that way. Most sought to waive some freshman courses, but stay the full four years.

At every juncture, Peterson was looking for ways to save money. Reducing the cost of writing and grading the examinations was a first priority, since the organization's only revenue came from the exam fees. All of its costs, other than what it received from the Ford grant, had to be met by whatever was left after it paid for the test processing. This net revenue figure was much less than zero in the early years, with few test takers and a very complicated exam. But in 1972 IBO achieved its first "profit," somewhat less than 10,000 Swiss francs, against total expenditures of 657,000 Swiss francs.

The next year an economic downturn hit the Western countries, and IBO faced financial oblivion. Inflation soared, exchange rates became chaotic, and financial support for public and private international initiatives dried up. Peterson began scrounging for grants and other forms of support. He received his most significant new commitment, $20,000, from the Hegeler Institute in the United States, the creation of businessman Blouke Carus, who had first read about IB in a short article in the *International Herald Tribune.*

Carus was a Caltech graduate who owned a chemical company and a publishing company in the Midwest and often traveled in Europe on business. He had long been interested in education, particularly as a publishing opportunity, and called the IBO office in Geneva after he read the article, but heard nothing back. It would be a while before Peterson met him, and saw how useful he could be in expanding IB in the United States.

Once the six-year IB experimental period had passed, and schools began to make long-term commitments to IB, reviews from professional educators began to arrive. "The IB is more demanding than the new German university entry qualification," said Eugene Egger, a member of the Swiss Commission of UNESCO. Paul Decorvet, director of the French Secondary section at Ecolint, said, "The higher level subjects are usually more rigorous than the same subject in the final two years of a national system."

Teachers and students said they liked the intellectual challenge and the emphasis on critical thinking, research papers, and oral examinations. The exams could be taken in either English or French, with Spanish added in 1982. The history course, many educators said, emphasized a non-national approach and had a good effect on attitudes concerning international cooperation, developing a real understanding of other countries' problems. In the United States, however, this created the suspicion among some parents and educators that IB was an undercover way of convincing innocent schoolchildren that they should support a world government and cast off old-fashioned ideas like the sovereignty and freedom of the United States.

There were also complaints about the educational nature of the courses. Some educators said the content of the subjects was too vast—the Theory of Knowledge course being a particularly ambitious example. This, the critics said, resulted in superficial investigations of significant topics. Some students said they did not like the limited exposure to the arts and sports. Students arriving at international schools from the United States found the second language requirement a huge challenge. It took at least three years to learn enough of a second language to pass an IB Language B requirement, and few American high schools required such a thing for their own diplomas.

Teachers and administrators also criticized the high cost, complicated administrative procedures, and communication difficulties with the IBO, particularly when their school was some distance from Geneva or Wales, where the IB examination grading operation had migrated.

To end formally the experimental period, the IBO held another major conference at Sèvres in April 1974. The news was mostly good. The sixty-four attendees from twenty-one countries recommended that the IB be made available in the greatest possible number of countries, with the widest diversity of cultural and educational traditions, including developing countries. The conference report noted that eighty international schools were on a waiting list to join IB after the experimental period was over.

But as good as the courses looked, IB as an organization had not solved its financial problems. The Ford Foundation grant expired in 1976. The UNESCO executive board decided not to assume the responsibility of keeping the IB afloat. In May of 1976, Peterson began a letter to all IB schools with these words: "It is with the most profound regret that I am compelled to notify all schools . . . that unless an additional $130,000 a year for the years 1977 and 1978 can be assured before July 15 of this year the decision to close down the project will be taken on that date. . . . If [negotiations] should prove unsuccessful, the IB office will close down on July 31 for all operations other than the administration of the 1977 examination and the completion of any separately funded development projects."

Several school heads protested, saying they could not allow the death of such an invigoration of their teaching. Ten educators representing schools that had been with IB the longest met with Peterson in his London office. Peterson was concerned about overburdening the schools, which had their own financial problems at a time of world recession. But when he suggested a school fee of 2,000 Swiss francs a year, in addition to exam fees, Charles Gellar of the Copenhagen International School said it had to be 10,000 Swiss francs—the 1976 equivalent of US $3,820—and all the other school heads agreed.

It was a difficult time for Peterson, but IB was doing so well in the schools, and had come so far on a shoestring, that he remained confident it would survive, no matter how catastrophic the situation sounded in this letter. In *Schools Across Frontiers*, he said he thought his feelings were well reflected in a farcical episode that occurred in 1976 as he was flying into Amsterdam for an important meeting.

The pilot said on the intercom: "I've just been warned that there is a bomb on this plane. I expect that it's just a hoax, as usual, but as a precaution we shall touch down on the edge of the tarmac, and I must ask you to evacuate as quickly as possible by means of the emergency chutes."

"This we did," Peterson recalled. "I had often wondered how they would work, and there was something splendidly childish about all the solemn bureaucrats and their wives, clutching brief cases and bags as they slid down the chutes like children in a playground. Everyone remained calm, even bored, with the exception of the air hostess who did not think we were taking it seriously enough and kept trying to speed up the flow of those collecting their belongings by saying, 'Hurry up. It's an emergency.'"

"Once out, we stood lethargically round the machine until someone suggested that if there really were a bomb on it, perhaps we had better move away," he said. "It all reminded me vividly of all of us in the IB, meeting one threat of bankruptcy after another over the six years with the continued conviction that somehow or other the final disaster would never happen. Nor did it."

With a system of increased school fees in place, the organization could begin to plan for serious growth, knowing the product they were selling was just what thousands of innovative educators around the world had been waiting for. That expansion put a severe strain on the test-scoring process, and led to the creation of a major administrative center outside of Switzerland.

The IBO presence in Britain at first had been the person of Alec Peterson, sitting and writing numerous letters in his office in Oxford and later London. The examinations had initially been handled, along with almost everything else, in Geneva. That was where the organization's heart was, as one of a number of international organizations working for world peace and cooperation.

But the cost of living in Geneva was astronomical, and if IBO was going to be supported entirely by member schools, it had to keep costs at a minimum. It was not drawing an allowance from the United Nations, like many of its Geneva neighbors. It needed to find a place where the rents were not so high. Peterson also argued that since most of the IB exams were in English, it would be good to locate that part of the operation in an English-speaking country and save the expense of recruiting English speakers to live and work in French-speaking Geneva.

Peterson thought the Language Centre at Southampton University might be a good location, at least for the grading of its language exams, which were by far the most complicated of all the IB tests to assess. The Language Centre's director, Tom Carter, had been head of languages at Atlantic College and an IB enthusiast. Not only was his center in an English speaking country with many educators capable of grading IB exams, but at a university that specialized in research on teaching languages and assessing fluency.

In 1974 IBO signed a contract with the center to rent space for the grading of its language exams. By 1977, IB was examining in twenty-four languages as Language A, the student's first language, and twenty-nine as language B, the second language.

IB exams were graded in both Geneva and Southampton until 1980 when Ruth Bonner, who had been in charge of exams in Geneva, retired. Marion Strudwick was appointed director of all IBO examinations, with her office in Southampton. By 1981 all IB examinations, except for languages, were administered from a new location at the Institute of Education, London University, where Peterson had been in 1976 to 1977 prior to his retirement as IBO director general, followed by deputy director general Robert Blackburn in 1978. Strudwick and most of her staff moved to London University in 1981. She was replaced by Derek Goulden in 1982.

The task became so large that in 1984 IBO moved all of its test grading to the University of Bath, where it occupied a top floor corridor in the northwest building of the university in that ancient resort town. By 1986 there were twenty-one people in the corridor, only three of whom had computers, and two more in the computer department in the basement of a separate building. The five IB computers were linked to the university mainframe. In 1988 IBO bought its own mainframe computer, which was huge and underpowered by twenty-first-century standards. There was no room for the data entry services—those were done at another office in the south of England that received the paper examination entries from the schools and produced the computer tape to send off to Bath.

That complicated system still did not meet the growing need for rapid grading of exams from a mushrooming list of schools. In 1989, finance and administration manager Tony Martell helped find new premises in St. Mellons Technology Park near Cardiff, Wales, for a relatively inexpensive rent. The entire IBO United Kingdom operation moved there in the same year.

By 1994, IB schools were registering their candidates electronically. In 2001 the IB United Kingdom office moved again into a much larger three-story building with 5,000 square meters of space in the Cardiff Gate Business Park. This provided adequate room for not only the test grading supervisors, but also the academic affairs department, which developed the curriculum and assessment tools for IB, the Middle Years Program, and the Primary Years Program, as well as business and finance, human resources, information and communication technology, and publications offices.

Hot Chocolate and
Peanut Butter

The International Baccalaureate program at Mount Vernon High School began on Tuesday, September 6, 1994, at seven o'clock in the morning. It was the day after Labor Day, a warm morning full of promise and uncertainty for the dozen educators assigned to make it work.

For the History of the Americas course, Glaze had decided that she needed to create the proper ambiance. She thought 7:00 a.m. was a horrible time to begin a difficult intellectual exercise. She absolutely had to have a cup of coffee if any thinking was to occur, and she knew many of her new students felt the same. So she turned her large classroom with big windows on the first floor into as comfortable and cozy an environment as she could manage. The first thing she made sure of was that there would be plenty of caffeine, and something to eat.

She befriended a helpful custodian. He found her some rugs and bookshelves and an old sofa and an even older easy chair. She made comfortable places for each student to sit. There was a big table in the back of the room with a coffee pot, a hot water pot, hot chocolate, bread, peanut butter, and jelly.

It being IB's first year at the school, and many students not wanting to take such an academic risk, the classes were relatively small. Glaze had three sections of History of the Americas, usually called HOA. Each had about fifteen students. She also had a regular U.S. history class, not part of the IB program. It was larger than her IB classes, but she had been teaching that subject for a decade and thought she could handle it.

There were adjustments she had to make. The classes at Jefferson had been on the block schedule, with each period ninety minutes long, meeting every other day. Mount Vernon would eventually adopt the same plan, but in 1994 it still had the traditional seven forty-five-minute classes meeting every day, and Glaze thought all that coming and going was going to kill her. At Jefferson, students nearly always came to class, making attendance taking easy. At Mount Vernon, Glaze had to keep track of absentees, and often found the school office aide eyeing her with exasperation when she found that Glaze had again forgotten to fill out the daily attendance sheet.

The students loved Glaze's carpeted learning nook, but they did not love the textbook. Neither did she. Keane's *Latin American History* was as dense as a Brazilian rainforest, and not nearly as exciting. "Mrs. Glaze," one student said, "it's not happening with this book." But the IB workshop leaders in New York had recommended it, so she was stuck, at least for the time being.

She was tossing her students into the deep end of the learning pool, and it was a struggle. They had very little background in Latin America. If Fairfax County had been in California, their elementary and middle school lessons would have given them some instruction in the arrival of Spanish explorers in the New World in the 1500s, the depredations of the Conquistadors in the Aztec and Incan empires, the blending of Spanish and native cultures, and many parts of Mexican history, including the founding of the missions by Father Junipero Serra, the Mexican War, the founding of the California Republic, and the rise of the Latino population in California, fueled by decades of legal and illegal immigration.

But in the standard Virginia curriculum, all that material was no more than a question or two on the fifth- and eighth-grade state history tests. So Glaze did what she had done in her American history classes with students who were similarly ill-prepared. She went over the reading bit by bit, helping them interpret the turgid prose and the many Spanish words.

"Did you read the chapter?" she would ask each morning. When she saw some blank looks—they may have read it but not understood it—she said, "Well, we'll read a couple paragraphs together and figure out what this guy's talking about."

She tried to make the chapter readings more palatable by using pre-reading strategies—talking about unusually difficult but important vocabulary words, displaying maps, giving the history a more modern interpretation, as if she were an embedded TV correspondent broadcasting Simon de Bolivar's latest battle. One day she even used the Mini Page, a feature for younger children in the Sunday comics section of the *Washington Post*, because it had a colorful map of South America with lots of interesting facts marked. She had the page laminated and posted it on her bulletin board.

Whatever the struggles of her IB classes, her regular American history class was much worse. These were the exact opposite of the students she had had at Jefferson. They were sullen, distracted, and not very appreciative of her enthusiasm for the topic. The white kids sat with other white kids, black kids with other black kids, Hispanic kids with other Hispanic kids, and so on. By the end of the year the class of thirty students, her largest by far, had lost twelve members to jail, pregnancy, and other mishaps.

The Mount Vernon plan, at least in the mind of Calhoon and Glaze, was to entrance these indifferent students with the magic of learning and lure them into IB. They wanted IB classes to reflect the ethnic mix of the school. The school board and the superintendent might have endorsed IB as a way to keep middle-class white and Asian families in the neighborhood, and in the public schools, but the IB teachers had seen enough examples of low-income black and Hispanic kids thriving in difficult courses to want to increase that number as much as possible.

The non-IB kids, Glaze thought, were much needier, and would soak up a better class if it were offered them in the right way. She noticed that when the IB students first arrived at her room in the morning, they would pour their little cups of coffee, or maybe make some hot chocolate, grab a pretzel, and sit down. The regular kids would plow through the drinks and snacks table as if they had not consumed any nutrients in days. They were ravenous. They would take at least three of whatever was there. It was like they couldn't get enough. She thought they needed more teaching, too.

15

Preparing Average Kids
for IB

Calanthia Tucker and other Mount Vernon faculty had discovered another program that, over time, helped prepare the school's neediest students for IB. It had been born in California, and was called AVID, for Advancement Via Individual Determination.

In 1980, an English teacher named Mary Catherine Swanson at Clairemont High School in the San Diego school district watched as dozens of new students from the low-income Hispanic neighborhoods south of the city's downtown were bused to her school. It was part of a desegregation plan and was voluntary. The only students who got on the buses were those who wanted to. But many of the teachers at Swanson's school were not happy about it. The south San Diego students were placed in remedial classes. Administrators worried that they might become discipline problems.

Swanson, on the other hand, thought they had potential, and wondered why more was not being done to help raise their level of achievement, since the whole point of busing them to that middle-class neighborhood was to give them a chance at a better education. As an experiment, she started a special class for thirty-two of them and called it AVID. She tried to teach them study skills and increase their confidence so they could take their places in regular and even honors classes, and grab the American dream that was so important to Swanson's upbeat view of the world.

She thought she was making some progress when a biology teacher, Mr. Brundage, confronted her angrily before school one Monday morning in December the first year of the program.

Jonathan Freedman's riveting book about AVID, *Wall of Fame*, recalled that the man was clenching a stack of tests in his hands.

"I demand your immediate apology!" he said to Swanson.

"What's the problem?" she said.

"Your kids cheated on the biology exam."

Swanson said she did not believe it, but Brundage said the evidence was irrefutable. He showed her a stack of tests taken by her students. All were marked with As or Bs. "Those kids could never master these concepts on their own," he said. "They must have done some, excuse me, 'group learning' while I was called out of the class."

Swanson was livid, but she controlled her temper. They agreed that Brundage would meet with the students and retest them any way he liked. When he arrived at the designated AVID class period, he began by giving Kouang, a Vietnamese refugee, a different test than the original examination, since Kouang's 92 had been the highest score among AVID students. On the new test, Kouang used the phrase "ontogeny recapitulates phylogeny," whose appearance on several of the AVID student test papers had stoked Brundage's suspicions of cheating.

"What does that mean?" he asked the boy.

"It says story of one creature repeat history of evolution of species," Kouang said. "But this old theory just gross generalize. Young people not have to repeat same old story of ancestors."

He grilled the other students in the room, who also kept their tempers because Swanson had told them to. Bernice, an African American student who was particularly angry, just answered the question, without expressing her true thoughts, when asked to trace the circulation system of a fetal pig.

"Your heart pumps blood from aorta to the lungs, where it picks up oxygen, and heads out to the organs and tissues," she said. "Then the veins carry back the carbon dioxide to the lungs, where it's exhaled. You know where Interstate 8 crosses the 5? That's the aorta of San Diego."

It took Brundage a while to check the retest scores and think about what had happened, but he came back and told the students and Swanson that he was wrong. "Based on my past expe-

rience, I didn't think you kids could do it," he said. "That was
my subjective opinion. But as a scientist, I have to rely on quantitative measures. The data have convinced me, beyond a doubt,
that you are innocent of cheating."

There was a gasp from the students. They were not used to
teachers admitting error. "Yes!" Bernice shouted.

"I misjudged you," he said. "I'm sorry. I won't underestimate
you again."

That was the turning point. A decade later, before IB arrived
in Fairfax County, Swanson's organization had become well-
known enough to convince Fairfax officials, including Calanthia
Tucker, that AVID might work in some of the Route 1 corridor
schools, like Mount Vernon. Tucker asked Joyce Jones, an
English teacher, to start an AVID class for ninth graders.

Jones's AVID class made progress, and was right across the
hall when Glaze set up her carpeted breakfast nook. Jones was far
ahead of Glaze in feeding hungry teens. Glaze accused her of
running a supermarket, with supplies of tuna fish and noodles
and Campbell's soup. When Glaze visited the class, the AVID
fourteen-year-olds would have their notebooks on their desks,
their pens and pencils ready, and their hands raised with questions. When they needed help, they came to see Jones after
school.

Glaze could sometimes hear Jones from across the hall, using
IB as a goal, a motivational device. The AVID freshmen had seen
the upperclassmen lounging with Glaze and holding lively discussions. IB had become fashionable, at least in their eyes, and
both Jones and Glaze knew they could use that. If someone lost
control, Jones would declare, "How do you expect Mrs. Glaze
to teach you if you act like that?"

When they finally reached Glaze's class as juniors, the AVID
kids would rarely be stars. They lacked the background of the
middle-class kids whose parents had Ivy League ambitions. But
they were thrilled with the idea of going to any college, since
they would be the first people in their families to do so. They
got Bs and Cs in their class work, but that was Bs and Cs in an
honors class, or even better in this case, an IB class. They were

happy about that. Their scores on the IB tests would usually be 3s and 4s, rather than 5s and 6s, but that too was okay with them.

16

Too Much Homework

The first year of IB at Mount Vernon High School would have a number of other challenges. There were, for instance, some teachers in the school who did not want IB at Mount Vernon and were still teaching AP courses.

Glaze understood their feelings. She had recently felt the resentment of having the administrative structure at Jefferson changed without much consultation with her. Whenever someone brought something new to a school, and some new staffers with it, no matter how nice they were and how carefully they chose their words, what many teachers would hear was: You aren't doing this right. You're doing something wrong. So we're going to give you something to replace it, and maybe we'll replace you too. The fact that Glaze was coming from Jefferson just made it worse.

Several factors helped Calhoon survive the ill will at faculty meetings and the sometimes hostile questions from parents who were friendly with the teachers who felt they were being replaced. The most important was Coleman Harris, president of the Parent Teacher Student Association. His daughter Ann was a good student, and he thought IB was just what she needed. He was the new program's biggest cheerleader.

Whenever Calhoon spoke to a community group, Harris would be there. He did much of the groundwork, making sure Tucker and the IB educator saw all the right community leaders. The middle-class parents were particularly supportive, making it much more jarring for Glaze when a few years later she had to handle an eruption of anti-IB venom from a much more affluent school, Woodson High, whose principal wanted to adopt IB. Those parents would sniff at the success that IB had at Mount Vernon and Stuart and say, dismissively, "Well, maybe it's okay for those schools."

They preferred AP, but at Mount Vernon AP was dying with almost no controversy at all. Harris and the other parents were convinced that as good as AP was, IB was better. A few of the AP courses survived for a few more years, but the students taking them were not as capable or as motivated as the IB students, and AP's demise had few mourners.

Glaze also had initial trouble with the workload she was assigning. The IB teachers shared their class calendars. Calhoon tried to make sure that everyone was not expecting major papers or giving important tests the same week. But classes often had similar rhythms. Final exams had to occur at the same time at the end of the report card marking period. Hell weeks could not be completely avoided.

Glaze thought one of her most important responsibilities was to make sure her students were ready for the 2,500-word paper, about ten pages, that IB called an "internal assessment" and would accompany the exams in history at the end of the year. She assigned three or four research papers a year, each of them ten to twenty pages long. This was five or six times the workload they were used to, and by the time the May final exam arrived she realized she had gone too far.

A few more papers of much shorter length would have served her purpose just as well, she eventually decided. She needed to get her students used to probing and analyzing the material, looking for weak spots and interesting corollaries of what they had found. But she didn't need to make them run a marathon every month.

She also had to stifle her instinct to encourage them in their pursuit of outside interests. She tried to make it clear that although they were certainly capable of handling the IB curriculum, they were going to need to reserve a large chunk of time each day after school to do so. Besides her history course, they were taking IB physics, English, art, math, and at least one foreign language. They were going to get at least two hours of homework a night, more than twice what they were used to, and they would often do much more than that.

They were ambitious students with a desire to have as many choices in life as possible. That was why they had decided to take IB. But that also meant that they were apt to want to play an after-school sport and run for student office and act in school plays. "Okay," Glaze said on many occasions. "You have to make some choices." She didn't have the power to restrict their lives outside her classroom, but if they were struggling she would talk to them. Often she tried to persuade them to drop at least one activity from their heavy schedule, and see if that helped.

At the end of their junior year, her students took a sample IB final exam. It was only ninety minutes long, rather than the five hours they would have to face in May of their senior year. She not only let them choose which essay questions they wished to answer, as would happen on the real exam, but had them work with her a week or two before the practice test to decide which questions she should ask.

She wrote possible questions on the board, both her ideas and their ideas. Then they thrashed over which made sense, which covered the material, which presented a valid issue that would stimulate productive thought and analysis. They were asked to behave as if they were the IB exam review committee. They not only loved the sense of power but realized that in thinking about what were the best questions to ask, they were reviewing the material and seeing its relative significance more clearly.

It was, Glaze realized, very much like being back at Jefferson. They were bright kids who were beginning to see how accomplished they were, and how much they could do if given enough encouragement, and time.

17

IB Comes to America

At the beginning, some people in Geneva did not think IB had much chance of success in the United States. American universities were, to be sure, the prime target of many IB candidates. American secondary schools, both private and public, had more financial resources than their counterparts in Europe, and the IB philosophy suited the thinking of American educational philosopher John Dewey, whose disciples ran many of the education schools and school districts in North America.

But IB was an unashamedly European product based on British, French, and German views of high school, notwithstanding its effort to be as international and inclusive as possible. There were some Americans among IB's founders, such as Leach, but they were international school teachers whose perspectives were very different from educators back home in the states.

The first three years of the post-experimental period did not show much potential for America. The numbers of schools using IB in Europe went from twenty-nine in 1977 to forty-one in 1979 and in Asia and Africa from twelve in 1977 to eighteen in 1979. In that period the number of North American schools increased from ten to twenty-four, what many onlookers thought was a puny number. In addition, those few IB schools in North America had very few students who did well enough to earn the IB diploma.

Then the situation began to change, as American educators, both private and public, began to hear what was happening in IB philosophy, language, and history classes in those few U.S.

schools that had taken the plunge. By 1984 the number of IB schools in Europe had jumped to sixty-six and in Asia and Africa they were up to thirty-seven, but the American growth was much more—to ninety schools in the United States and thirty-six in Canada, the North American total being larger than the rest of the world combined.

This growth did not come easily, said those who made it happen. The IB founders were uncertain how to handle the program in the United States, and did not get it right immediately. The first few American IB schools were all private, but were not the mainstream preparatory schools, like Exeter and Collegiate and St. Albans, that had educated the sons and daughters of the wealthiest Americans for decades. The first IB schools in America were UNIS, the Anglo-American School in New York, the French-American School in San Francisco, and the Washington International School in the District of Columbia, whose director Dorothy Goodman became one of the most outspoken advocates for IB in the country. To those were added two of the United World Colleges, internationally oriented college prep programs inspired by Peterson's mentor, Lord Mountbatten, in this case the Lester B. Pearson United World College of the Pacific in Canada and the Armand Hammer United World College of the American West in New Mexico.

Peterson recalled in his book the initial failures to make IB big in the states. First, he and Harpo Hanson tried to persuade the brand-name prep schools, including Phillips Academy Andover and Phillips Exeter Academy, to introduce the courses. The teachers at those schools were interested, and Andover spent money on a serious study of IB, but in the end they concluded, as such schools usually did when contemplating reform, that there was no sense in fixing a problem that did not exist. They had some of the best teachers in the country and the highest level of success in getting their students into Harvard, Yale, and Princeton. Their students did well on the AP, which had been originally designed just for them. They wished Peterson and Hanson good luck, but did not sign up. The same thing had happened when Peterson tried to sell IB to the English equivalent of Andover and Exeter—boarding schools such as Eton, Shrewsbury, and Uppingham.

A second but equally unsuccessful approach was the effort to establish IB in American community colleges. These inexpensive and usually public two-year colleges were designed to prepare students for the workplace with technical courses or for transfer to four-year schools by providing the introductory liberal arts courses that most four-year college freshmen and sophomores took. Since IB was itself a liberal arts program, and more rigorous than what was found in most community colleges, its organizers thought this might be a good fit.

Seymour Eskow, the president of Rockland Community College north of New York City, was the principal advocate of this approach. The IB North America office was created in New York in 1976, and in October of that year Eskow addressed a meeting of its board of directors. He said of the three prime attractions of IB—its rigor, its attractiveness to U.S. colleges, and its connections to education overseas—the third one was the most important to community college administrators. He wanted to give Rockland students a chance to study abroad, and it seemed to him that if they started IB courses at his school, they could continue with the same program at IB schools overseas.

Unfortunately, the idea did not work in practice. Rockland IB students, and IB students from Mercer County Community College in New Jersey, who also participated, were not happy with their year at Hammersmith and West London College, which had agreed to receive this new breed of American IB students. Peterson, who was working at Hammersmith and West London at the time, said, "We did our best to give the Rocklanders a welcome and an international experience, but I don't think we realized how great the culture shock would be, nor how much careful planning and special attention would have been necessary to make a success of this first experiment."

Some high schools tried a different kind of experiment with IB in community colleges that also failed in the 1970s, only to be revived later. Twenty-two high schools in ten states made it possible for talented eleventh graders to skip their twelfth-grade year and go directly into an IB program at a local community college. They received their high school diploma at the end of their first year in the program, and their associate of arts degree at the end of the second year, qualifying them to transfer to their junior year at a four-year college one year sooner than they would have under the regular system.

Coordination between the high schools and the colleges proved to be clumsy, and many high schools opposed a program that would rob them of some of their best students during the senior year.

What did work for IB, and far better than its European designers had hoped, was the use of the program as a way to invigorate and revitalize public high schools that, in the 1970s, were beginning to realize that they were producing too many thinly educated graduates not ready for college. By the 1980s, as a series of national reports decried the lack of rigor in public education, even some inner-city high schools saw IB as a way both to improve their teaching and keep or attract middle-class students whose parents were tempted to move to better neighborhoods or place them in private schools.

18

Slow Response from Geneva

Blouke Carus stumbled across IB almost by chance, when he saw a three-inch story in the *International Herald Tribune* in 1970. Business for his firm, the Carus Chemical Company based in Peru, Illinois, required that he visit Europe two or three times a year, and he was a regular HerTrib reader. The item caught his eye because he had long been interested in the state of American education, and wondered why European students were so much more serious about their studies than the young people he knew in the United States. He wanted to reconceive secondary education to be more rigorous and to build upon the European experience, including middle school.

He wrote a letter to the IBO in Geneva, introducing himself and asking for more information. He said he thought he might be able to help them establish themselves in the United States. He invited the IBO to send someone to speak to the advisory board of his publishing company, Open Court (the publisher of this book).

There was no answer. He wrote again, still no response. Later he learned this was typical. Gérard Renaud was a brilliant educator in Carus's view. But the philosophy teacher was sometimes overwhelmed by the details of running a growing organization, and answering the mail was something he did poorly.

When Carus heard that Alec Peterson was executive director, he wrote directly to him. Peterson responded quickly, but was very cautious. He met with Carus several times to see if he was serious. Eventually he decided that Carus was just the sort of practical internationalist that he needed to expand the IB franchise. They organized a meeting at UNIS in December 1973 for interested people, and IB's North America operation began to take shape.

Carus was born in Chicago to a midwestern business family active in both chemicals and publishing. They were very well traveled and as an adult Carus could not get over his memories of studying for a semester at a Gymnasium in Germany in 1939 when he was eleven. The German students were studying Latin and doing daily writing exercises and acting as if this were what all boys their age did. When Carus returned to the United States it was the same as always: his peers in La Salle, Illinois, were into sports and parties, not school. He wondered: Why was the environment so different?

Carus's launching of *Cricket* magazine and the success of his Open Court phonics-rich K-6 reading program were part of his plan to alter the American curriculum and youth culture. He was convinced that the seventh and eighth grades in the United States were disasters. The middle schools and junior highs were repeating sixth-grade lessons, marking time until their students were old enough for high school, while their European counterparts were getting deep into algebra and foreign languages and science.

He thought it was stupid to wait until ninth grade to start serious instruction in foreign languages. First graders could be learning to sing songs in French and Spanish and German, and the lessons could grow more sophisticated with each new grade in elementary school. He remembered how difficult it was to learn German as an adult, when he did graduate work in chemistry at the University of Freiburg from 1949 to 1951.

He thought American schools, public and private, were insular institutions that did not want to hear about their flaws, and were particularly deaf to complaints from parents like him. He was active in the PTA in La Salle, halfway between Chicago and Peoria, when his children were in school in the 1960s. He learned that educators did not want parents to have anything to do with academics, other than making sure their children did their homework. If parents wanted to raise money for the school with a bake sale, that was fine, but the crucial decisions about what was to be taught had to be left up to the administrators and teachers, whom Carus came to regard as a secret cabal that was not up to the job.

He understood the reasons for this. The neighborhood school and the local school board had been part of American culture since the first few public schools had begun in the nineteenth century. What he thought was an isolated system was perceived by most Americans as independent and accessible. American politicians recoiled at the control Europe's national education systems had over their student assessments, and there was not much Carus could do about that.

But he was going to try anyway, by helping IB establish itself in North America. After the initial meeting in December 1973, Carus helped organize the first board of directors for IB North America and became chairman two years later. The Carus contribution was funded with a grant from Carus's Hegeler Institute, what Carus referred to as "our little insignificant institute." The new board hired an executive director and installed him at Rockland County Community College, where the doomed experiment with introducing IB to America via the two-year colleges was already underway.

The IBO needed a board incorporated in the United States and an American infrastructure in order to have a chance of raising the funds that would be needed to train American teachers. But the effort did not go smoothly. The North American organizers had an idea of what they wanted to do, but it was always difficult to hire staff with low salaries and nothing more than a mission statement to tell the new employees what the enterprise was all about. The board had a rapid turnover in executive directors before IB North America got to the point where everyone knew what they wanted to do.

After Carus hired Gilbert Nicol, an attorney with extensive experience in university administration work, as executive director in 1977, the administrative chaos diminished and more got done.

But there were still regular conflicts between Geneva and New York about money, a bureaucratic squabble that Carus called "one of the most ridiculous things you have ever seen in your life." Carus, less prone than some of his European IB friends to romantic notions of international understanding, was also dubious about the Geneva headquarter's approach to the United Nations, and its frequent attempts to seek funding, and even become a part of UNESCO. In a May 1976 letter to a potential donor in Chicago, Carus called UNESCO's decision to deny IBO's request for $140,000 "a blessing in disguise." He said, "Now UNESCO will have no controls or authority in IB affairs."

Carus liked Nicol because the new executive director, a title that was eventually changed to regional director, realized the importance of the expansion in America and kept at it. Nicol was very demanding and not easy to work for, but to Carus he turned out to be a doer, and very effective.

The experiment with community colleges disintegrated quickly, and the board and Nicol looked instead for high schools that would like to try IB. This was greeted with great skepticism by people inside and outside IB North America. Harvard College administrator David A. Hartnett, a member of the IB North America board, said in a January 17, 1977, letter to board members that "perhaps the whole venture is really not viable in North America, except at a few international schools" and suggested the full-time IB office in New York "be phased out." William W. Dunkum, chairman of mathematics and science at T. C. Williams High School in Alexandria, Virginia, wrote Nicol a few months later that IB's costs and the competition from AP meant no more than twenty students in a typical American high school would ever participate, and that was not enough for the program to survive.

But Carus, Nicol, and the board persevered. Their strategy was to use UNIS to sell the program in the United States, since the New York school was one of the original IB schools and could show IB school prospects how it could be done successfully.

The UNIS faculty and administrators had the same missionary zeal as Carus and Nicol and were eager to help. IB officials, sometimes with UNIS teachers, traveled from coast to coast, holding conferences at places like the Wingspread in Racine, Wisconsin, San Francisco, and Florida, and inviting teachers to visit UNIS in New York. The word spread.

Treating Plato Like
Michael Jordan

As the second year of IB at Mount Vernon High began, there was no longer any room in Glaze's teaching schedule for regular kids. She was given three classes of History of the Americas, now expanded to thirty students each, plus one Theory of Knowledge class with fifteen students. She loved getting a chance to teach TOK. She shared Calhoon's interest in philosophy—they had both grown up intrigued by the intellectual foundations of their nation's democracy—and looked forward to talking about Plato and Aquinas and Kant.

Calhoon could not run the growing program and still teach three sections of TOK, so she gave one class to the English department chair, one to Glaze, and kept one for herself, a small treat to save herself from a sad life of nothing but administrative duties. All three TOK teachers saw the course as the intellectual glue that bound all the IB courses together. What do we know? How can we know it? What is the nature of this thing called language by which we share what we know?

Glaze kept looking for new ways to make this work for teenagers. She showed excerpts from the film *Nell*, starring Jodie Foster. She left out the nudity and other parts that might bother parents, and instead let students see how the title character, a young woman who had been left to raise herself in the woods, had developed her own language, and how it fit the world she knew.

There was a great deal of journal writing in her class. Glaze started the day by putting a question on the board, or a quote from the works of one of the thinkers they were studying, and asking them to record their reaction. She wanted IB students to be thinking freely, and connecting what they learned in one class with what they learned in the next. She often stayed late, sometimes until 7:00 p.m., to make sure her agenda for the next day's class was ready, with the kickoff question on the board. Not being a morning person, this gave her a head start on the next day.

The portion of African American and Hispanic students in her classes had increased about 20 percent in a year. Most of them were still non-Hispanic whites and Asians, but Mount Vernon's effort to coax more minorities into honors and IB was having an effect. Glaze was convinced that once a student new to these classes saw that they only needed to put in the time to do well, they adjusted rapidly. What were these smart kids doing that they couldn't do? They were asking questions. They were expressing personal opinions about what they were reading. What was so hard about that? Once the so-called marginal students got a taste of the sights and sounds of an IB class, they saw it was not so mysterious or intimidating as they had thought.

Glaze pushed for a looping system for the two-year IB courses. Looping was the teachers' lounge term for staying with the same group of kids for more than one year. It had become popular in some elementary schools. The teacher who taught a group of first graders to read often proved to be the best person to handle any problems that developed as they tackled more difficult words and sentences in second grade. Glaze thought this also made sense for two-year IB classes, like History of the Americas.

She had handed off her juniors to Carol Wonsong for the second part of the course, leading to the big exam in May of the senior year. Glaze had absolute confidence in Wonsong, but she thought the students might appreciate the continuity and familiarity of having the same teacher for both years.

The IB faculty at Mount Vernon saw room for improvement after the first two years of the program. The first year their students had taken 74 exams, with 68 percent scoring 4 or above. The second year there were 251 exams, with only 62 percent scoring 4 and above. Physics was still struggling, with only 10 out of 33 exams scoring 4 and above, for an average score of 3.09.

But far more students were taking the college-level courses and tests than had ever taken AP at Mount Vernon, and the program was continuing to grow. The same thing was happening at Stuart, leading the county to accede to requests from other schools for IB. Glaze would eventually take a new job to coordinate this growth as specialist for advanced academic programs in the county, overseeing both AP and IB as Fairfax County became one of the largest givers of such tests in the country.

Glaze had lots of stories to tell teachers who wondered how to make this work for every student, not just the self-directed kids who were already deciding which Ivy League schools they would attend. One of her favorite memories was of Kevin and Duc, two basketball-crazed boys in her Theory of Knowledge class.

They had been among the students who had to be strongly urged to take IB against their strong desire to have a relatively easy academic life. After just a few days, they told Glaze that all that talk of Kant and Aristotle and other white guys with no jump shot made their brains hurt.

Glaze had long experience with the likes of Kevin and Duc, who either enjoyed pretending they were not smart or actually believed they were intellectually deprived because many of the people in their neighborhoods did not do well in school. Kevin was African American and Duc was Vietnamese American, but their ethnicity was not, Glaze thought, their problem. She knew them better than they knew themselves. They were bright young males with a reluctance to work all that hard, and one day she caught them being much smarter than they pretended to be.

The two were talking about an NBA playoff game, analyzing, judging, synthesizing, what-if-ing. "Listen to yourselves!" she said. "Your brains know what to do. Just treat Plato as though he were Michael Jordan!"

That got them. They could not deny the truth of what she had said. And so they started to get into the course, still complaining, but jumping into discussions as if they were scrambling for the ball, exploring the big ideas. They were proving, as the IB staff at Mount Vernon had hoped, that high school could be more than an effort to keep easily distractable adolescents quiet and comfortable until graduation day.

A Rookie Teacher Tries IB

Emmet Rosenfeld thought he would be hired full time at West Potomac High School, Mount Vernon's nearby rival, in the fall of 1992. He had graduated from West Potomac just six years before, and although he was only twenty-four, he had a bachelor's degree in English from Harvard University and a teaching certificate from the Harvard Graduate School of Education. Most important of all, he had already been teaching at West Potomac as a long-term substitute, making a name for himself with a special cycling program for at-risk ninth graders.

But he was wrong. The school did not hire him full time. Perhaps someone at West Potomac still remembered the less attractive part of his record as a student there.

During his senior year, Rosenfeld had been co-president of the student body and helped his old school Groveton High School merge successfully with its often unfriendly neighbor Fort Hunt High School to create the new West Potomac High. He had helped pick the West Potomac mascot and school colors and made what might have been a difficult year go smoothly. But some administrators also recalled his junior year when he and some friends, not all of them sober, had broken into the school building and done some damage. His part was rather innocent—putting some mice under a box to frighten the security guard—but one of his fellow perpetrators had vandalized a teacher's room and Rosenfeld had to do sixty hours of community service.

Since he wasn't going to work at West Potomac, he accepted a job teaching English at Mount Vernon High. The school's

English department chair told Rosenfeld, a sweet-tempered and expressive young man with long brown hair, that he remembered Rosenfeld's big sister Becky, who later became a public defender in New York City. She had been half of the legendary Groveton High debating team of Becky and Becky that had crushed a Mount Vernon team. Rosenfeld was inexperienced in what to say and what not to say in an employment interview, but his ideas for experiential learning, like the log cabin he had had one of his classes design, were the kind of thing Mount Vernon was looking for, so he was hired.

Rosenfeld was assigned a collection of ninth-grade classes, including an English as a Second Language class. From the start he had trouble following the rules. He did not keep careful records of who was tardy. He often overlooked the ban on students wearing hats. When he sent some of his class outside for a project, and was told other teachers had complained of the disruption, he said, "Well, why can't they send their kids outside too?"

But he was a natural teacher. Even in high school he had been a soccer coach and camp counselor. In college he took time off to teach swimming to kids in remote Alaskan villages, and then became an Outward Bound instructor. While still an undergraduate he signed up for an accelerated program that earned him a teaching credential in his senior year and allowed him to avoid having to write a senior thesis in the English department. Gradually it occurred to him that he might actually make a living in the classroom. He had fun with special projects for students, like the assembly of national flags he organized in his ninth grade ESL class.

When Rosenfeld first heard about the IB program at Mount Vernon, he dismissed it as another political stunt, a school board pretense of concern about this low-performing school. But when the English department head asked him if he would be willing to take the IB twelfth-grade classes, he said fine. He wanted to try something different, and there were parts of the IB program that impressed him.

He decided it was not an elitist program for white middle-class kids, since Mount Vernon did not have many such students and the courses were open to anyone who wanted to try them. And he liked the fact that they were actually going to give him some training. That did not happen very often.

He went to a week's IB training session in Atlanta during the summer of 1995, traveling with an eccentric French teacher who gave him a lift to the airport, but stopped with her husband along the way to buy a car, as if they were just running into a supermarket for milk. It was the first time he had gotten any kind of legitimate professional training since he became a teacher. Both the training and the style of the IB English courses fit his biases about the best way to teach. The Atlanta training had been less lecture-driven than the UNIS training that had annoyed Glaze, and that was a good start for Rosenfeld.

There would be no fill-in-the-bubbles multiple-choice tests in IB, he was happy to see, for such exams were very high on his list of things to hate. IB would not demand that he make sure his students could name four Dickens novels and five modes of literary interpretation and be ready to mark the right circle or box on the tests. Instead, his students would be assessed on the basis of papers, essay test questions, and oral examinations, and there was a fairly wide choice as to which books they could read.

Rosenfeld, a novice teacher, was being given twelfth graders because the IB English program would take two years to prepare students for the May of senior year tests, and it was considered easier to take students who had already had a good year of IB as juniors than to take raw recruits from the tenth grade and give them the shock treatment of a thick IB reading list and a steady diet of writing assignments.

Also teaching IB English was another recent Harvard graduate, Jay Locher. Rosenfeld and Locher had both attended Fairfax County high schools. Both were self-confident instructors and both wore their hair in pony tails.

But Rosenfeld was destined to stay in the Mount Vernon IB program much longer than Locher, and develop a feel for teaching kids from non-college families that would grow stronger because of the many ways the program, and his Mount Vernon supervisors, allowed him to try new things without warning him against taking too many risks.

Raising American Standards

Experimentation, many IB founders said, was what the program was all about. Peterson had emphasized IB as "a test bed for innovation—a useful possibility of experiment with new developments in curriculum and examinations which it would be difficult to try out within nationally-controlled systems." Several countries took this toe-in-the-water approach to the new program, designating one or two schools as IB laboratories and watching closely to see what happened.

But most of those countries, unlike the United States, had strong central government control of their public schools. In his memoir, Peterson concluded that the prime reason for IB growth in the United States was that "there was no central control of either the curriculum or the standards of achievement."

"In a country as enormous as the U.S., with an almost infinite variety of school districts having considerable control over the secondary school curriculum, those responsible for the tertiary stage of education, beginning with such colleges as Harvard or Columbia, clearly needed some criterion of admission which would at least screen out such applicants as were manifestly incapable of following academic courses," Peterson said. "The alternative could only have been selection by nepotism or wealth.

"This screen was provided in Europe by examination systems, more or less centrally controlled, which, by their very nature, controlled the curriculum," he said. "The Constitution of the United States ruled out such a single Federal system. . . . It was left, therefore, to private initiative."

That gap was filled, somewhat incompletely and awkwardly, by the SAT and ACT exams, but they were general tests of reading, writing, and mathematics that did not apply directly to what was taught in high schools, particularly in the last two grades before graduation. Most American high school students did not take them anyway. This lack of accountability produced a common complaint among American high school teachers and administrators, what they called the senior slump. By the last term of high school, with required courses completed and college applications sent, seventeen-year-olds saw little need to spend much energy in class, and did not do so.

One solution was the creation of the Advanced Placement program by the College Board in the mid-1950s. Like the IB, it was the fruit of decades of concern about a problem that, at first, affected only a small number of students. At the beginning of the twentieth century, the deans of Harvard College discovered that many freshmen had already learned some introductory college material in preparatory school. Why not give them a special test in that subject, it was suggested, and allow them to skip the college course?

To make what would eventually be called the AP examination convenient, three test sites were provided the summer before matriculation: Cambridge, Massachusetts, the university's home; Quincy, Massachusetts, an exclusive Boston suburb; and Paris, France, for those spending their fathers' money on the Grand Tour.

A few other private colleges began similar programs, but the idea did not go far. After World War I, American educators focused on creating a standard high school curriculum for every youth, rich or poor. They had little time for elitist notions like Advanced Placement.

During World War II, many U.S. college administrators noticed remarkable results achieved by wartime crash courses for young men and women who needed to absorb detailed technical data and languages in a very short time. After the war, as scientific learning expanded rapidly and left the standard high school and college curricula far behind, a large number of

American educators began to wonder if they were missing something.

In the mid-1950s, before Harpo Hanson became head of the College Board's AP program and a member of the IB North America board, he was an assistant dean at Harvard. He and deans he knew at other colleges noticed that many of the strongest students coming from private preparatory schools seemed to lose momentum in their freshman year. Research showed that when college-level courses were offered in secondary schools, the need to repeat the same material as college freshmen led to boredom and surprisingly poor grades for otherwise accomplished students.

So a few colleges and secondary schools decided to revive and extend AP. From its infancy, the program held a silver pencil in its hand. It was a device to relieve the boredom of a few bright high school seniors in extremely wealthy or unusually competitive high schools. The plan was that those schools would offer college-level courses to a few students. The colleges, with the help of panels of experts, would create special examinations to prove the students did not need to repeat the same material. If they passed, they would receive college credit.

The 104 secondary schools who participated in the first AP examinations in May 1956 included Andover, Exeter, Groton, Deerfield, the Bronx High School of Science, New Trier, Bethesda-Chevy Chase, and Cranbrook.

The College Board, originally known as the College Entrance Examination Board, had been set up by a few select colleges in 1900 to provide a way to test college applicants before deciding whom to admit. It created the SAT, originally called the Scholastic Aptitude Test, and in 1947, with the American Council on Education and the Carnegie Foundation for the Advancement of Teaching, set up the Educational Testing Service (ETS) to administer the SAT and a growing number of other tests.

By the time the AP program began, the College Board was well aware that its membership had grown far beyond the Ivy League. It agreed that any AP test would be open to any student who wanted to take it. Some educators accepted this decision reluctantly. Certainly, they acknowledged, the AP program should not be just for schools with pedigrees going back a century. But no one expected it to move far beyond that privileged domain.

One Harvard admissions officer guessed that 120 high schools might eventually participate. Feeling optimistic, Hanson wagered the maximum would be 220. But he did not anticipate the Sputnik crisis, and a succession of reports that said American high schools were not adequately preparing their graduates for either college or jobs. The result was an explosion of interest in AP. Instead of 220 high schools participating in the program, by the beginning of the twenty-first century there were nearly 14,000.

Arriving in America two decades after AP began, IB rode the same rising tide of dissatisfaction and appetite for more rigor. Peterson thought the three most immediate causes of IB's early growth in the United States were this dissatisfaction with teaching standards in high school, plus the fact that IB now had a financially self-supporting office in New York and that the new executive director for North America, Nicol, launched a series of very effective introductory seminars and teachers' workshops when he took office in 1977.

One of the most important reform documents of the 1980s, a report by the Carnegie Foundation for the Advancement of Teaching called "High School," recommended a tougher high school program that sounded very much like IB, including a public service requirement similar to the CAS and a senior independent project similar to the IB extended essay.

American high schools that adopted IB were happy to have a tested curriculum that seemed to fit the new national mood. Many were run by ambitious principals who wanted to distinguish their schools from those joining the much larger AP program. The magic of IB for Americans, Peterson said, was "a coherent curriculum based on a positive, though flexible, concept of education, a sense of excitement for both students and teachers deriving from participation in an international cooperative project and a challenge deriving from matching themselves against international standards."

Daniel Tyson, a teacher at the Armand Hammer United World College of the American West, made the distinction at that time: "Why introduce the IB to challenge good students when the AP program already provides this opportunity? One answer is the kind of challenge each provides. It is one thing for students to prepare for AP examinations in subjects they like and do well in. It is another kind of challenge to prepare for external examinations that cover an entire curriculum, integrate one's learning in the Theory of Knowledge course, write an extended essay and perform community service."

Just how that kind of sophisticated teaching would work with students who were not accustomed to it, like many of the new IB participants at Mount Vernon, remained to be seen.

One Big Question

Rosenfeld, while preparing for his first twelfth-grade IB English classes, noticed that the essay tests and papers and oral examinations would be almost entirely focused on literary analysis. There was no canon of specific works that his students had to memorize so that they could identify which quotes were uttered by which characters, a standard assessment device at private schools and public schools in the wealthier neighborhoods.

They needed to learn a way of thinking about literature, a way of talking about it, and Rosenfeld boiled that all down into one interrogative statement.

"I am going to tell you the two most important questions in the IB program," he told each new class. "How does it make you feel?"

There would be a pause of anticipation in the room, and when the teacher said nothing more, a student would usually raise a hand. "Mr. Rosenfeld, that's only *one* question."

"'How does it make you *feel?*' is the starting point," he told them. "In other words, what is your emotional response to this piece of art? That's the starting point, and you can have a legitimate personal response."

"And then," he continued, "*how* does it make you feel? In other words, how does the author use literary techniques and language itself in order to create this emotional impact?"

He liked IB for the *how* part, because it made students into critical readers. Instead of simply learning how to find the metaphors, the similes, and other devices in a homework assignment, something that a computer could do, they were forced to talk about how the author used language to create this impact.

The English department head would occasionally make it seem that Rosenfeld and Locher were just barely surviving in his department. They were rookies and deserved some abuse. Each year in the spring, when the next year's IB staff was being decided, he would tell Rosenfeld, "I just managed to keep you, you know."

But Rosenfeld found himself enjoying IB. He had a clear map of what his year was supposed to look like, for one thing. He knew generally what the IB test would require, and what written assignments were expected. For IB Language A, which meant his English class, half of each student's year-end assessment would depend on two long essays they would have to write during the exam, so he focused on that kind of writing in the second half of the year. Thirty percent would depend on the oral exam and 20 percent on two papers they would do at home, the world literature assignments or WLAs.

The assignments were clear, but that did not mean they were easy. The 1,000 to 1,500-word literary analysis papers they would have to write were the equivalent of Mount Everest for his students. They were also reading about eight books a year, and some of those works were very challenging, such as *As I Lay Dying*, *The Bluest Eye*, *Miramar*, *Wild Geese*, and *A Tale of Genji*.

The English department chair tried to keep Rosenfeld under his wing the first few years, making sure he didn't get lost in the intricacies of exams and lose the joy that he thought should be a part of any literature class. Rosenfeld would let him look at what was going on, but he soon concluded that he had his own style, and he wasn't going to change it as long as it worked.

When Rosenfeld was moved to eleventh-grade IB English after two years, that was the signal that the rookie had arrived. He became the anchorman, the person whose lessons would set the tone for IB English instruction and deeply affect how the students would do in twelfth grade as well as eleventh. Staff turnover was a problem, and Rosenfeld would often be the one asked to introduce new teachers to what they were doing.

When he was a new teacher, his main concern was how to get through each day, but after a few years he found himself stepping back and allowing himself a longer look. He had always been very project oriented. He thought one of the reasons he had been hired was that he had built replicas of sod houses for a history class for special education students at a previous school. Some of the feedback he had gotten from IB readers was withering, and some was picayune, like the reader who said his students did not put proper headings on their papers. But he could be confident that there were few schools as diverse as his in the IB universe that had 103 kids taking an IB English test, as Mount Vernon had in 2003, with the average grade being 4.45 on the 7-point scale, with fifteen 6s and 7s and no grades below 3.

He invented something called spinning plates, a way to engage an entire class in an exploration of literary themes by breaking the class into small groups and allowing each group to read the required books in any order they chose. They would all read the same book at the beginning of the course, and then each group of about four students would draw up its own reading schedule. If one group wanted to read *The Great Gatsby* while another was reading *The Color Purple*, that was fine.

Everyone in class would keep a daily journal of their thoughts on whatever they were reading. They would have class exercises that forced them to confront the differences and similarities between what they were reading and what the other groups were reading. Rosenfeld would, for example, ask each group to pick a pivotal passage from the book it was reading. They would have to make a case for why that passage was so important, mark the passage with a different color for each literary device, maybe do a poster about it and present their work to each other. It was a way both to challenge their own analyses and to get a sense of what the rest of the reading list held in store.

Rosenfeld became a very different teacher than he was when everyone in class was on the same page of the same assignment. If they were reading different books, it made no sense to ask them what the light in Act 3 of a Shakespeare play symbolized. The students would have different opinions, and they often thought that literature was so flexible that all opinions were valid. That, Rosenfeld thought, was often nonsense, and one way to prove it was to ask leading questions that would make sense to all the students, no matter what book they were reading.

"What do you think was important here?" he asked. He was confident of his abilities as a literary interpreter, and could switch from one book to another with ease. It was fun to get students to make new connections, some that even he had not seen in works that he had thought were thoroughly familiar to him. And he came up with a few new ideas himself.

Some other teachers thought spinning plates was going too far. "What do you mean?" one asked. "How could you not teach a book at a time?" But once he started to do more than one at a time, he realized it would be hard for him to ever go back.

The IB emphasis on crossing from one culture to another and making connections pushed him further in that direction. He taught a lesson, for instance, on *iki,* the Japanese concept of love. His students learned that there was no such thing as falling in love to many Japanese. They *grew into* love, and his students had to get used to that, the old Japanese concept of marriage being something best arranged by families with the two individuals in most cases comfortable with the idea of making adjustments to make the union work and eventually developing a deep regard for each other. Rosenfeld tried to help them see that that attitude extended to other forms of art, and other cultures.

The lessons on *how* the work made them feel also required a different way of teaching. There was, as in all literature classes, an emphasis on literary terms, but Rosenfeld tried to make these concrete to teenagers who in their previous English classes had only been asked to get the characters and plots right.

"You're a carpenter building a house," he said. "You don't take your hammer and hold it up in the air and say, 'This is a hammer! Look, I've got a hammer!' In the same way, we don't need to shout 'This is a metaphor!'"

"But what you do is you step back when you're done and say, 'Look at that! Look, I framed it, and look at the house, how it all came together.'"

The idea was to get them to speak the language and use literary terms effectively, but in the context of the whole plan of the book, not just isolated identifications that would get them a point on a multiple choice test.

23

Geneva and New York Fight about Money

The first American public high school to adopt IB was Francis Lewis High School in Queens. The principal, Mel Serisky, had read a news article about the program, heard more at a conference on gifted education, and visited IB classes at UNIS. In 1977 he told Peterson he wanted the program in his school. He said he had "programs for the ethnic, programs for the handicapped, programs for the deaf, programs for the semi-literate, special programs in computing, but no program for the brightest students aiming at the best colleges." He and his teachers were happy to entertain visitors from other public schools, just as UNIS had done for private schools, which helped many educators understand what IB was about.

IBO leaders in Switzerland and England were happy that the new IB North America organization could raise funds in the United States and Canada from local businesses and foundations, without having to tap Geneva's meager bank account. Leading the effort to put the American IB on a sound financial footing was Carus, whose family's Hegeler Institute grants had been essential.

Peterson liked Carus not only because he was such a force for change in American schools but also because he organized such interesting conferences. Peterson recalled his delight in stumbling upon people he would never otherwise meet at these meetings, such as an old man he met in the lobby of a Starved Rock, Illinois, conference held by Carus. "We spent a very pleasant and to me fascinating hour walking round the gardens and talking, but without introducing ourselves," Peterson said in his memoir.

"Indeed, for all we knew, either of us might have been the janitor; when we checked in it turned out that he was Isaac Bashevis Singer."

Carus, as the chairman of the IB North America board, saw IB as a way to toughen and deepen teaching at the high school level, but it needed a strong organization and a missonary zeal. The first IB North America regional director at Rockland Community College had been Howard Berry. The next director was Charles Rose, a Renaissance art historian who agreed to occupy the first small office, rented from the College Board under a Hanson arrangement for only $125 a month, on a temporary basis until a permanent director could be found. Rose was a specialist in the history of Venice and went there nearly every year. He spoke excellent French, and served two years.

His successor, who took office in August 1977, was Nicol, who had served in American military intelligence during World War II and then had a successful career as a university administrator, including stints raising funds for Princeton and serving as executive director of the Society of College and University Planning. There was talk of establishing a permanent IB office at Harvard or UNIS or the College Board, but the Americans recommended a permanent and independent office in New York City.

They found space at 680 Fifth Avenue, but could afford only 200 square feet, partitioned off from the reception area on the ninth floor. It reminded Peterson of his similarly tiny office at Hammersmith and West London College, and he was impressed at how much Nicol got done in the limited space. After six years the office moved to larger quarters at 200 Madison Avenue.

Nicol was a chain smoker who sometimes walked out of major IBO conferences for a cigarette in the lobby. He lived in Greenwich Village and was stubborn in professional matters—his fights with Geneva were legendary—but very charming if you spent an evening with him. His protective feelings toward the infant schools he was nurturing in America were so strong that when Georges Laforest, chief examiner for IB philosophy and Theory of Knowledge, visited the United States in the late

1970s, Nicol told him he could not enter any of the new IB North America schools.

Laforest visited them anyway—he knew Nicol had no money for security guards to keep him out. And as Nicol expected, the Frenchman did not like what he saw. He told Renaud the TOK lessons were sloppy at many schools, but not at UNIS, where Sue Bastian was setting an international standard for that unique and challenging course.

Some IBO officials said Nicol was just what was needed to get IB started in America. He was willing to take chances on schools that might not be able to reach the international standard, just so the organization could survive financially. A wheeler-dealer, he sometimes discounted the annual fee for some schools just to get them on board, even though he had no authority to do so. Once a school was in the group, he worked hard to raise the level of its teaching with workshops and seminars.

Peterson was annoyed to discover that some IB participants took IB North America's Fifth Avenue address, and the business acumen of key backers like Carus, as a sign that IB North America was swimming in dollars while the rest of the organization starved. But both the North American and European offices of IB had serious cash-flow problems in the late 1970s, and their financial disputes were based on more than just misimpressions of each other's resources.

Geneva and New York could not always agree on how much of the fees paid by the growing number of North American IB schools would be sent to Europe to help pay for operations there. The exchange rate between the dollar and the Swiss franc continued to fluctuate, exacerbating these arguments. Their first agreement in 1975 said that IB North America could keep all school subscriptions on its turf and spend any foundation money it raised in North America, but would pay the IBO for all North American testing fees. The next year the IBO executive committee insisted on a fifth of the North American school subscription fees.

In 1980 Carus turned his chairmanship of IB North America over to Tom Hagoort, who had helped found the Washington

International School and relocate UNIS. Carus said he wanted to have more time for IBO Council of Foundation business. In February 1981 the first annual IB heads of school conference was held in the United States, and much built-up resentment toward the North American organization poured out.

The day before the conference, Renaud warned the IB North America board that he was hearing growing concern about "the potential Americanization of the IB program." The next day the headmaster of an IB school in Asia told Peterson that he and several other principals had decided that the present allocation of funds between Geneva and New York would either kill IB altogether or force a complete takeover by the Americans. It was difficult to persuade anyone who had not seen the salary schedule, or the cramped Fifth Avenue office, that the Americans were not living in luxury on IBO's money, but a meeting of the IBO management committee later that year, with Carus and Hagoort in attendance, worked out a special grant of 20,000 Swiss francs from IB North America to IBO, and the crisis subsided.

At that meeting, Hagoort said that if IBO was to become financially viable without repeated begging for more money from the foundations, it had to establish many more schools, and North America seemed to have the greatest growth potential. There were a limited number of international schools around the world. The European public schools were mostly under the grip of national curriculum policies and were not comfortable with competition from the IB. Only the freewheeling Americans, with every district and sometimes every school picking its own curriculum, could provide enough new school subscriptions to keep IB afloat.

In 1981 IBO published a plan for equal revenue from three sources—examination fees, school subscriptions, and government contributions. But by 1985 school subscriptions were providing 51.5 percent of the money, with examination fees providing 27 percent, publications and workshop income 11.2 percent, and government contributions only 10.3 percent. "There can be little doubt," Peterson said, "that without the 300 percent growth of North American IB schools between 1980 and 1985, a period when the number of IB schools in the rest of the world grew by approximately 33 percent, IBO as a whole might have foundered."

Mr. Rosenfeld's Students

Rosenfeld could be creative in ways he had not been before because the IB English test, and thus the course, was not content driven. His students did not have to memorize every character and every plot twist. As they discussed the themes he raised, he thought, those facts became a natural part of what they learned.

The students and he could have fun with the material. He had them pick a scene from Hamlet and either submit a video of themselves performing it or act it out in class. That gave them a sense of how different the same scene could be when different directors and actors got their hands on it.

He organized the Existential Olympics after they read Albert Camus' *The Stranger*. This was during the slack time in May that followed the IB tests, when he could be playful without anyone worrying that it might hurt test preparation. Each group had to create a game related to existentialism or *The Stranger*. Rosenfeld's favorite was the game that required the participant to sit with his mouth stuffed with marshmallows and try to read lines from *The Stranger*, making the point that communication was often impossible in an existential world.

Rosenfeld found that his IB English classes were the ones most likely to attract students who were the least certain they wanted to be in IB. They took an IB course or two to see if they could handle a college-level challenge. There were 100 to 150 juniors and seniors taking IB English for just the certificate—more than any other IB discipline. Rosenfeld was happy that despite what might be their inadequate preparation before they arrived in class, the techniques he and the other IB English teachers used produced good scores on the IB test, with 85 percent getting at least a 4, enough for college credit.

Those who entered IB selected themselves, and those who dropped out did so too, more or less. Rosenfeld had a name for the dropouts. They were the "I was" group. Many students would sign up for twelfth-grade IB with Stacia Zeimet, head of the English department, after completing an unsuccessful eleventh-grade year with Ds and Fs. They wanted to stay with their IB friends, but unless they made a significant effort to improve their attitude and effort, they were not allowed back in.

The English department chair gave Rosenfeld the incoming IB juniors, but also assigned him regular classes to take advantage of his touch with less-motivated teenagers. Rosenfeld's last year at Mount Vernon, before he switched to a private school to avoid the Virginia state tests he so loathed, was 2002-2003. That year he had three sections of regular eleventh-grade English, about twenty-five students per section, and two sections of IB eleventh-grade English, a little more than twenty in each section.

His IB classes had a higher percentage of middle-class students with college-educated parents than the student body as a whole, but many of his students had parents who had not attended college. The percentage of minorities in his classes was only slightly below their percentage in the school. In a regular English class of twenty-five students, he would typically have about ten non-Hispanic white students, five Asians, five blacks, and five Hispanics. Ascertaining their family backgrounds was sometimes difficult, but the parents of the African American and Hispanic students had usually not completed college.

He let his reading groups organize themselves. That often meant students picked classmates of the same ethnicity. One group during his last year was typical: five students of African descent, whom we shall call Roland, Daniel, Jasmine, Traci, and Sasha.

Roland was a football player, and his family recent immigrants from Haiti. He was a B student and a good worker. He wrote things down. He was well organized. But at the beginning of the class he had no idea how to structure a paper. He just started putting sentences on paper, and did not know how to edit his work into something coherent.

Rosenfeld helped him make paragraph outlines and experiment with topic sentences. Gradually his work improved, mainly because his good work habits carried him forward. He handed in a couple of papers with obviously plagiarized passages, but when Rosenfeld told him that that was not right, he stopped doing it.

Roland's closest friend in the group was Daniel. Like Roland he was an athlete, on the track team, and seemed to have stronger academic skills than his friend, particularly in writing. But his study skills were not as good. He made a good first impression. He spoke well and was respectful of Rosenfeld, which led the teacher to think Daniel was from a military family. But by the middle of the year he was often coming late to class and forgetting assignments. He did not participate much in class and sometimes fell asleep.

Given his academic skills—his scores on the state achievement tests were higher than Roland's—he would have gotten Bs easily in the regular courses. He continued to be respectful in class and would usually produce the required work, but long after the deadline. Rosenfeld gave him a C, and urged him to get organized. Roland got a B, and kept improving.

Jasmine was a lively young woman who was on the cheerleading team and had the ability, Rosenfeld noticed, to switch from standard English to inner city patois as the situation demanded. She had the ability to get an A, Rosenfeld thought, and always did her work on time in his class, so it surprised him when the cheerleading coach said she did not think Jasmine was as reliable as he did. She got a B-plus in Rosenfeld's class.

Traci and Sasha, the last two in that group, were different from the others. Traci's family had emigrated from Ghana, and she did not do well in IB English, getting mostly Ds and Fs. Sasha had no recent foreign background in her family, but she also did not do much work and got bad grades. The two of them were regularly complaining about the way Rosenfeld treated them, telling him that they deserved a gentler approach.

"You know, we're different," they told him. "Don't you understand? We're not like these other kids." They were "ghetto," they said. Their parents did not have the same ambitions for them that the parents of the other students in their group seemed to have, and although they were clearly intelligent enough to learn something in IB, they came in with poor reading and writing skills and did not seem very interested in improving them.

Rosenfeld was particularly annoyed at their habit of chatting in class when he was trying to make a point. "Traci, Sasha," he said, "I need you to stop talking while I'm talking and look at me." That annoyed them, and they would punish Rosenfeld by being even more defiant.

Sasha had a quick mind and some writing skills, but rarely did her assignments. Traci was better organized, but struggled with the material. Rosenfeld gave them some leeway. He was supposed to fail anyone who was tardy nine times, but he didn't do that in their cases. He was not good at keeping track of tardies and sending the required letters home to warn parents, so he just took what little they gave him, and asked them to do more.

"I think you guys can do this," he said to them in a private pep talk. "You know, all you need to do is do your work. I mean, it's different when you come in late and you don't do your work like all the other students."

Eventually the bottom fell out for Traci. In the third quarter, everyone was supposed to make an oral presentation. It was a major part of their grade. They had done a lot of work on their presentations in class, but Traci had missed many of those days. And when the day came for her presentation—pushed to the very end of the unit to give her more time—she did not show up. She came to the next class with a feeble excuse and handed in what she said was a paper to substitute for the oral presentation, but it was so bad Rosenfeld did not even bother to grade it.

That was the final act in their battle of wills. Rosenfeld told Traci she was going to have to come to him and formally request that he reschedule her presentation, or give him a believable explanation of what had thrown her off schedule. But she did not do that. So he said to her, "Look, you've got an F, but if you want to change your grade, all you've got to do is come and, basically, apologize and be decent about it." She never did. She took the F and did not return to IB the next year.

Traci and Sasha were in IB because a teacher or counselor had seen their quickness and their intelligence and suggested they try it. Even though they found the work difficult, and could not organize their days to complete the assignments, they seemed to feel a certain pride in being IB students. They had friends there, and an image to protect, so they had hung on, even though they were never comfortable with the demands IB placed on them.

In other classes Rosenfeld had other students with varying approaches to college-level learning. His second period class was often livelier. Students did better in the morning, before lunch. One student, who can be called Steve, was Hispanic, very nice and personable, if a little lazy in the usual teenage way. He might occasionally miss one of Rosenfeld's deadlines, and then two days later hand in the required paper, which would turn out to be in fine shape.

In the same class was Cindy, who was also Hispanic, and always well dressed and well organized. She was a class officer and a good listener. Her mother would come to one of the morning touch-base meetings—teachers made themselves available on designated days to any parent who dropped by—and Cindy would interpret for her, since Rosenfeld's Spanish was nonexistent.

Another student in that class, Dominique, was African American, and proud of it. She was a good student, but needed help with her writing.

Steve and Cindy were capable of doing IB quality work. Cindy had excellent insights into characters but did not quite know what an analytical paper should look like. She turned in one paper that had a huge block quote from the book, almost a page long. It was not the thing you would find in the work of a student with any academic savvy.

So Rosenfeld took her through it. This is how you present a close reading, he said. You have this passage, and you talk about the passage afterwards, and this is the way you format the paper.

He also worked with Dannie, a sweet girl with African immigrant parents, who worked hard but struggled with the material. Rosenfeld thought she would have been better placed in a regular English class, but she preferred to get a C or D in an IB class, and work with him to improve. She was not intimidated or depressed by the low grade. She liked the fact that she was surrounded by better students, and thought she would learn more that way. Perhaps in every class two or three students would fit that profile, the opposite of slackers. They were strugglers who were happy to have more work at a higher level than they could handle.

25

IB and Rigor in America

Carus had seen his business grow and had the same hopes for IB. During his first visit to Geneva, he declared that someday there would be a thousand IB schools in the United States. He could see that the Europeans thought he was a dreamer, but he intended to make it happen, and knew there were many American educators who shared his dissatisfaction with the U.S. public education system and wanted something more rigorous.

Liberal education, he told all who would listen, was in trouble in both high school and college. He believed strongly that a genuine liberal education was only possible if the foundations were laid in secondary school, as in the European systems. Unfortunately, everything was being slanted toward getting students ready for jobs and professions. The great thinkers and great books were being ignored. When he visited the president of his college alma mater, Marvin Goldberger at the California Institute of Technology, he said: "Marvin, I will wager you that less than 5 percent of the graduates of Caltech could pass the IB exams."

"You're probably right," Goldberger said.

Caltech students worked until midnight every night on an assortment of science and technology courses. Most of them did not have time to take a foreign language, or learn how to write, or study the humanities and social sciences.

Carus's argument, used by many IB advocates, lured more and more high school principals and teachers to IB seminars and training sessions. The program also received a significant boost as more colleges saw how well grounded the new crop of IB diploma holders were.

Cliff Sjogren, the University of Michigan director of admissions, encountered IB in 1973 when Nicol asked him for help in getting his university to recognize the program. Sjogren was also chair of the National Council on the Evaluation of Foreign Educational Credentials, and had many programs from overseas cross his desk. He sent the IB course outlines to a few Michigan faculty members, assuming they would find nothing useful and he could get on with council business. But to his surprise they not only said they would recognize IB for credit, but suggested he start recruiting IB students for Michigan.

After talking to them and taking a closer look himself, he sent a letter to eighty-six international schools around the world. He often visited such schools and was happy when he began seeing his letter posted on many bulletin boards. It said:

> The best predictor of academic success at Michigan is previous academic performance. Students who elect and satisfy the standards of a rigorous and demanding academic program in high school are the ones best suited to benefit from the intellectual environment of the University. A transcript that reveals a student's enrollment in International Baccalaureate courses serves notice to the admissions officer that the applicant is someone who accepts rather than avoids educational challenges. Further, a successful International Baccalaureate student will enroll at Michigan with some advantages over students who have taken less intensive programs. The educational sophistication that students develop through an experience in an International Baccalaureate Program will serve them well at Michigan and other institutions that attract serious students. Other advantages include an increased degree of self-confidence that comes from classroom experience with college-level academic material, a sharing of intellectual activities with the best students of the school, better time management, more experience with independent study, and a unique experience in "learning how to learn" through the Theory of Knowledge course. Of course, the fact that the International Baccalaureate is a world examination with near universal recognition can mean additional benefits for the internationally oriented young scholar.

Secondary schools also benefit from their sponsorship of the International Baccalaureate. The quality of the school from which the applicant graduates is a factor in admissions decisions at the University of Michigan. A major criterion in the assessment of a school's quality is the level and quality of courses that are offered to the college bound population. Above-average grades in a very good school are looked at more favorably than superior grades at a mediocre school. Unquestionably, a school that graduates each year a number of students with International Baccalaureate diplomas has demonstrated its commitment to high educational standards and that commitment will serve to influence admissions decisions at the University of Michigan.

The International Baccalaureate program is uniquely designed to serve intelligent, serious students and progressive secondary schools that seek to create or maintain high educational standards. The University of Michigan is proud to be an active participant in International Baccalaureate activities with these students and their schools.

Such a letter from a brand-name university had great power, for by the 1970s colleges were dictating much of what was being taught in U.S. high schools. American politicians had long defended the notion of local control of public schools, and denounced the idea of a national curriculum as found in many European countries. Education in the United States was funded mostly by local and state taxes—the federal government provided less than 10 percent of the money—and local voters, represented by the people they elected to school boards, should make the curriculum decisions, most American policy makers thought.

But educators and journalists who visited schools in different parts of the country in the 1970s and 1980s as IB was getting started scratched their heads at the notion that Americans lacked a national curriculum. The pace and order of the lessons were more or less the same no matter where they went. American high schools usually taught U.S. history in the eleventh grade and U.S. government in the twelfth grade. The science courses were taught in this order: biology, chemistry, and then physics. Algebra was a ninth grade course, except for a few exceptional students who might take it in middle school or junior high.

Why? Because that was what they had been doing for decades, and few educators, except very contrarian critics like Admiral Hiram Rickover, suggested changes. Whatever the local congressman said about the wonders of federalism melted in the heat of parental desires for their children to get into a good college. The major universities all had very similar entrance requirements, so the public school—and private school—course lists looked very similar.

Once college admissions officers like Sjogren saw how well IB students were doing when they got to their campuses, they began to praise the program and admit more IB graduates. This in turn caused more high schools to embrace IB as a way to distinguish themselves and make sure the most college-conscious families moved into their neighborhoods and sent children to their schools.

Carus saw the high school hunger for IB as a reaction to the low standards of American secondary education and the tendency toward overspecialization by AP students. The College Board program did not require that the teachers be trained for AP and did not push for students to take AP courses in every core subject, as the IB diploma program did. A strong math student might take AP Calculus, but he was less likely to take AP English Composition. A strong foreign-language student might take AP French, but was less likely to take AP Chemistry. To Carus this meant that even in strong AP schools the students never got a broad education. IB, he told everyone, was several levels of sophistication better than AP and laid the foundation for a liberal education, not more specialization.

American school districts also began to show some interest in IBO programs for younger students, although the two school models that emerged, the Middle Years Program (MYP) and the Primary Years Program (PYP), were very different from IB and at the beginning much less popular. Like the IB diploma, both were conceived by loose-knit coalitions of educators impatient for schools better than what they had.

Some of the ideas in the MYP and the PYP can be traced back to some of the IB founders, particularly Cole-Baker, although it took several decades for the pre–high school programs to become part of the IBO family, and IB officials emphasized that they were in no way prerequisites for IB. In 1966 the International Schools Association published an International Primary School Curriculum edited by Cole-Baker. It listed seven subject areas and stressed using exploratory teaching methods, with an emphasis on John Dewey's project-driven approach.

In the early 1990s, ISA published a program for students aged eleven to sixteen. Without an infrastructure to support it, ISA decided to offer the program to IBO, which accepted it in 1992 and entitled it the IBO "Middle Years Programme." It was offered to schools beginning in 1994, after IBO made several changes in the original structure.

What the IBO was to call the "Primary Years Programme" had a similar history. Under the name International Schools Curriculum Project, a group of educators developed a program for students aged three to twelve. ICSP had neither an office nor a staff, so they offered the program to IBO, which began making it available to schools in 1997.

PYP and MYP were less sharply defined than IB, and not as different from standard elementary and middle schools in the United States as IB was from standard high schools. They did not grow as quickly, although the MYP succeeded in winning a U.S. Education Department grant in 2002 to help expansion, and IB North America officials predicted each would be in more schools than IB by the end of the decade.

Carus thought the most immediate selling point for the IB in the United States was what eventually brought the program to Mount Vernon High School. Many urban and inner-suburban schools that had once had fine reputations saw their middle-class students move to the outer suburbs to escape what they perceived as declining standards. What was actually happening was an increase in the portion of low-income students at those schools, including more young people from immigrant families where English was not the first language, but that did not necessarily mean that there was no room for a college-level curriculum. College-oriented families in those neighborhoods sought some proof of serious efforts to keep standards up, and IB was a vivid way to do that.

Rufus King High School in Milwaukee was one of the first to use IB successfully in this way. Eventually several other large cities put IB into urban schools with impressive results. The *Newsweek* magazine list of America's most challenging public high schools, created by Jay Mathews and published in June 2003, had five IB schools in the top ten: International Academy in Bloomfield Hills, Michigan; Stanton College Prep and Paxon, both in Jacksonville, Florida; George Mason in Falls Church; and Myers Park in Charlotte, North Carolina. Three of the five— Stanton, Paxon, and Myers Park—were urban schools that had acquired IB in part to stop the flight of middle-class students to suburban and private schools.

There were several other schools like that on the list, including Richard Montgomery in Rockville, Maryland; St. Petersburg High in Florida; Enloe High in Raleigh, North Carolina; Eastside High in Gainesville, Florida; and Wilson Magnet in Rochester, New York. And many more started to talk about applying.

26

Thinking in the Fishbowl

Rosenfeld had an assortment of devices to keep his IB students engaged in what were often complex and multilayered pieces of literature. There was, for instance, the fishbowl, a way of presenting and analyzing difficult passages by having each group take a turn being the center of attention, sharing their thoughts with each other while the rest of the class looked on.

The class sat in a circle, and each group in turn entered the fishbowl, the middle of the circle. Rosenfeld distributed passages they had chosen for analysis. The class took notes as the group in the fishbowl talked, and asked questions at the end.

It was better than putting one student on the spot. If the group members were together in the bowl, they could handle it. They had to bring five ideas—Rosenfeld called them "golden apples"—into the fishbowl to get started, such as an observation about a character or a link to something else they had read. He would leave them in the bowl for fifteen minutes or so, sometimes allowing another student to dive in and help. He sprinkled some fish food—suggestive ideas of his own—in the bowl if they seemed to need that.

Working on writing, on the other hand, was a very different process. It was on an individual, case-by-case basis, and very time consuming. Rosenfeld conducted workshops in class to address writing problems in each group. He handed out drafts of classmates' work. They proofread them and looked for flaws, the kind of peer editing encouraged by the National Writing Project. But Rosenfeld often found that ineffective. They did not have time to go over all the papers in class, and the student suggestions were often not very helpful.

So he tried to make the workshops less structured. Bring your draft to class, he said, and find someone to help you or work on it yourself. He called them to his desk to add his thoughts or schedule meetings after school.

For the world literature assignments (WLAs), the process became very structured. Those papers counted in the formal IB assessment. The students submitted a draft, Rosenfeld made comments—although the rule was he could not mark the paper—and the students would rewrite.

Stimulating thoughts about literature required imaginative approaches. He had them do one paper in the style of Laura Esquivel, author of *Like Water for Chocolate*. They had to find recipes important to their families, and then bring them in for a live writing exercise. He projected his PowerPoint screen on the wall and talked about how to brainstorm such a paper. He would write on the screen. They would watch him do it.

He asked them to think about the persons in their families with whom the recipes were associated, and they would follow his lead. "Okay, physical characteristics, I want three of those," he said. If it was a recipe for Aunt Fern's Chocolate Pie, they had to describe Aunt Fern. Was she fat or thin, tall or small, long hair or short? Did she wear glasses? How old was she?

He wrote on the screen his notes on the character he was describing, and gave them a few minutes to fill out their own note sheets. Then he would move to the next topic, such as, what were some funny things that this character had said?

It was a lesson in pre-writing. They watched how he did it, and then tried it themselves. It usually worked well, he thought. They acquired so much raw material in those pre-writing sessions that it was hard for them not to produce an interesting paper, and some were adapted for the IB's world literature assignment requirement.

They did many short writing assignments, what Rosenfeld called reader responses. They made notes on the eight novels and plays that they had to read over the course of the year. Each reader response was supposed to fill about two pages in their journals. Sometimes Rosenfeld would read them, or have students read each other's. Sometimes, when time was short, he would just check off that they had been done.

They took poems and color-coded them. Each literary device—a metaphor, a simile, a tense change, a voice change—was highlighted with a marker of a different color. A few papers were about real events, like their essays on the anniversary of the September 11, 2001, attacks. He had each student bring in a 9/11 news item, post it on the bulletin board, and use it to inspire their thoughts.

To prepare his students for the IB exams, Rosenfeld had them practice writing timed essays. The exercise was brutal because the test had to be handwritten. Most of his students, even those from less affluent families, were accustomed to having word processors and knowing that every letter they typed could be easily read.

The sample test questions often asked them to compare other books to a certain reading passage. Rosenfeld advised them to use what he called the helicopter effect: "You have to be able to go way up high over the book you are discussing, give us a good global look at it, and then zoom down to a place that is directly relevant to the point you are making." They had to be able to operate at different levels above the text and move easily between them. It was hard for them to visualize their audience correctly and provide the right amount of context.

He said, "Picture an intelligent outside reader, an adult reader, who may not have read the book recently, or be familiar with the book." Experienced writers knew when and how to summarize a book in a sentence or a paragraph, but the inexperienced writers in his classes tended to go on and on with their summaries. When writing the world literature assignments, that was a big problem. It was crucial that instead of just repeating what they knew, they met the test makers' demand for analysis and an argument. Giving them a large question that required them to select from among the works they had read was high-level synthesis, very difficult for sixteen- and seventeen-year-olds.

They had to find a starting point and fire a persuasive arrow of thought that landed somewhere.

Experienced writers were accustomed to thinking as they wrote, not even knowing what they might say in answer to a question until they started writing. But in an IB exam, the clock was ticking and these young amateurs were more likely to panic and freeze up. They lacked the confidence that they would come up with a meaningful idea. Rosenfeld tried all the latest methods for training students to think. He had them construct a web of different talking points, each thought in a circle and connected to other circles by lines. But even with all the practice at planning, trusting their ability to finish the piece before the proctor said "Time!" was hard for them.

Under IB rules Rosenfeld was not allowed to mark their drafts. At the beginning he did not like that rule, and often violated it, but eventually he accepted, somewhat reluctantly, the IB notion that students had to learn to fix flaws on their own. Inserting changes red-penciled by their teacher would not help them do that.

He thought that students would learn better if he edited the stuffing out of their papers, forced them to confront all of their mistakes and bad decisions, and then have them redo the work. But he was an IB teacher so he did it the IB way, sort of. He kept a separate sheet of paper beside the draft being discussed and wrote down comments: "Page 3, paragraph 2, rewrite to reinforce your point."

He admired other IB teachers' workhorse energies. Rosenfeld had done the arithmetic. If he spent ten minutes with every student's paper, and had three classes, that was sixty students, or six hundred minutes—ten hours of editing. Just thinking about it exhausted him, but older teachers seemed to enjoy it. They had lots of ideas that added even more work to their schedules. The English department chair would sometimes tape his comments and hand them to each student, saving time since he could talk faster than he could write. He held individual after school conferences with every student, getting home very late.

As the years went by, Rosenfeld became more comfortable with student work that was imperfect, but more true to their thinking than it would have been if he had torn it up and ordered its reconstruction. He demanded somewhat fewer writing assignments because he feared being worn down to nothing by the workload.

A School That Dumped IB

Bernie Glaze did not immediately realize that she had a crisis at W. T. Woodson High School, one of the Fairfax County schools that followed Mount Vernon and Stuart in adopting IB.

As the county specialist for advanced academic programs, working in a satellite administrative office near Route 50, she was used to getting calls about college-level courses. When Woodson parents began calling in 1999, she thought it was more of the same. She was the only central office administrator who had taught an IB class, so she got a lot of questions about the program. And people knew she was a very friendly woman who would do her best to help.

The Woodson questions sounded innocent enough. But she began to notice that once she gave them the basics on IB, these parents would often respond, "But isn't it true that. . . ?" And ask about reports that IB was not honored by colleges, that it was just for low-income students, that it was not in line with state or national mathematics standards.

No, she said, the college admissions offices loved IB and were more likely to admit a student who had taken IB courses, but, yes, their academic departments were not as familiar with the program as they should be and often gave, without understanding why, the same credit for a one-year AP course that they gave for a two-year IB course unless the IB student had gotten the full diploma. The program had been designed for the very best international students, and its use to engage low-income students at a school like Mount Vernon was relatively new, but had proved successful in many cases. The math courses were different from the AP math courses, but they met all the standards, and were preferred by some math professors who liked their more creative approach.

What was happening at Woodson, Glaze learned, was a full-fledged anti-IB revolt. The Woodson principal had gone through the usual IB approval process, with participation from teachers and the school's Parent Teacher Student Association, but many parents had thought that IB was just a nice addition to the school's already strong AP program, rather than its replacement. By the fall of 1999 the principal had left the school for reasons unrelated to the controversy and a new principal had to sort it all out.

Fairfax County in 1999 agreed to pay for the first time the test fees of every AP student, and at the same time require them to take the AP exam if they were in an AP course, just as was already required of IB students. This caused the number of AP tests taken at Woodson to nearly double in one year, from 435 in 1998 to 788 in 1999. The passing rate on the tests dropped from 81 percent to 65 percent, but that was still above the national average and both parents and students were pleased by the increased participation in a college-level program.

The new Woodson principal, Robert Elliott, learned that many parents were just beginning to realize that this blossoming AP program would be mostly supplanted by IB under the school district plan. There was not enough money to support both programs, county school officials had decided, and every high school thinking of switching to IB was told it had to choose, except for Robinson Secondary School, which was unusually large and could support both programs. At Woodson, there were almost as many people who wanted to switch to IB as wanted to keep AP, and that meant several months of sometimes ugly arguments.

Many parents saw no reason to change the strong college-level program they already had. And to some of them, IB looked like a scam, or at least an uncertain quantity. It had been created by Europeans whose school systems were different, they said. Only a few hundred American schools had tried it. The two Fairfax County schools that had first adopted IB were very different from Woodson, a mostly middle-class school where the percentage of students on free and reduced lunches was less than 10 percent, compared to nearly 40 percent at Mount Vernon.

Parents had many fears and concerns, and they dumped them on Bernie Glaze. A less experienced teacher who had seen first-hand what IB did for students at Mount Vernon might have lost her temper and condescended to the Woodson parents and teachers. But Glaze had spent eight years at Jefferson High, where the self-regard of the students and parents was unequaled in the United States. She was accustomed to dealing gently with people who thought they were smarter than she was.

"How does IB compare to AP?" a parent asked.

"Well, you know, I've taught at Jefferson. I've taught AP. I've taught IB, and it's absolutely rigorous, it's absolutely challenging."

"Isn't it true, Mrs. Glaze," one parent said, "that the colleges really prefer AP, and you're putting all of our kids at a great disadvantage in college admission?"

"Well," she said, "that's not my experience of that, but if you really want to know the answer to that, go to the college web pages, and they all have their AP and IB policies out there."

She went to parent meetings at Woodson with Nancy Sprague, the assistant superintendent for curriculum and instruction, and Janie Smith, the director of high school instruction, who was Glaze's immediate boss. Glaze told the parents what she knew from being an IB teacher. She told them what their children would be getting, in terms of content and rigor. But it was clear to her that many people were not convinced.

Elliott, the Woodson principal, convened a committee of teachers, parents, and students to study the issue—with a roughly equal number of IB and AP advocates—and solicited input from the entire school community. The topic inspired passionate opinions, with articulate proponents on each side, but as the discussions continued the pro-AP side seemed to be in the majority. Some parents said that the IB program forced students to make hard choices among offerings, and perhaps threatened their chance to participate in Woodson's large music and arts program. Some said that the IB curriculum had too much of a global perspective, and downplayed American history. Some said that the AP program had been successful and that there was an insufficient rationale for replacing it. Some said that they were bothered by the lack of college credit for individual one-year IB courses, even if the credit would be granted to students who received the IB diploma.

Glaze was glad that she did not have to run the meetings at Woodson. She was just there to answer questions. The debate among parents and teachers was not pretty to see. It had turned into a political battle, with each side convinced of the rightness of their cause. Both AP and IB were quality programs, she knew. Either would serve the students well. But the Redskins and the Cowboys were also good football teams, and that did not dilute the venom fans hurled at one another.

Members of the committee visited a total IB school, George Mason in Falls Church, and a school that had both IB and AP, Washington-Lee High School in neighboring Arlington County. They voted overwhelmingly for keeping both programs, but when told this was impossible, the final vote on Nov. 22, 1999, was 15 to 10 in favor of AP.

One of the most influential statements before the vote came from Susan Shue. She was a former AP Government and IB Social Anthropology teacher at Mount Vernon High. When she transferred to Woodson in 1997, she taught the same two courses and became the school's AP coordinator.

She was reluctant to take sides with so much division on the issue, but at a critical moment she spoke out. She identified several areas of strength in both programs, but also said that if a decision had to be made, her choice would be to retain AP.

One of the pro-IB parents on the committee, John Buescher, who had worked at the National Endowment for the Humanities, later explained in a memo to the committee why he voted for AP. "I still believe that the IB program is a more rigorous, richer, more pedagogically sound curriculum," he said. He said he rejected the argument "that the AP program is more 'patriotic' somehow or that the IB program is tainted because it is 'foreign.' . . . I get knots in my stomach when I hear people playing this tune to rally support against the invasion of our curriculum by folks that are just not like us.

"My AP vote," he explained, "meant that I was persuaded that the largest part of the Woodson community did not support the IB program and could not be led to do so. We were asked to vote on which program was a better fit for the school. I did that, and by voting AP, I made a political judgment about the community, not a judgment about the merits of the programs. On the other hand, I believe I contributed to healing a rift between the school and the community that could not be healed (in anything like the short term) in any other way that I could imagine."

The committee and Elliott made sure that students who were already enrolled in IB classes could continue until they graduated. E. J. "Nell" Hurley, one of the Woodson parents who led the pro-AP side, noted that the controversy only seemed to strengthen the school's participation in college-level courses. By 2003 Woodson had students taking 1,331 AP tests, one of the largest programs of any school in the country. On the *Washington Post*'s list of the most challenging public schools in the region, also created by Mathews, it placed seventh out of 157 schools, with the highest AP/IB participation rating in Fairfax County except for Jefferson.

After the Woodson controversy, Fairfax administrators took more care in making sure that community members understood what a switch to IB meant before they introduced the program. Glaze was convinced that the more information people had, the better off they were. And if they didn't want IB, that was fine, she thought, because other schools would.

With IB courses in eight of the county's twenty-four high schools, the questions parents asked Glaze became very different. Most of them were not from families with high schoolers, but middle schoolers. They wanted to know how they could get their fifth, sixth, or seventh grader ready for these college level high school courses they were hearing about, and which did she think was the best program.

"You have to decide as a family what to do," Glaze told them. "And the only way you can decide that is to get as much information as you can, sit down and talk about the impact of more homework, more difficult exams, and different rhythms and requirements in each program."

She told them whatever they decided it was going to be a lot of work. She asked them to think about how they were going to handle the "Oh my God, I can't do this" crying sessions that were common with teenagers coming into contact with AP or IB. Sometimes the phone conversations with these parents would go on for an hour.

She could see the program maturing as more parents and teachers became accustomed to IB and its demands, and she loved to hear stories of students for whom the program had done just what it promised.

28

Ordering the Class Ring

Christin Roach and her family moved to the Mount Vernon neighborhood because of IB. Such an event would not have occurred at the beginning of the program, but by 1997, when Roach arrived at the school, IB had acquired a luster that was affecting property values and relocation decisions.

Roach's father, Frank Roach Jr., read about the Mount Vernon IB program in the *Washington Post*. It sounded to him, a minister with a master's degree in divinity, like just the thing for his daughter.

She was a good student and was always placed in the gifted programs of the Maryland and Virginia schools she attended. They were living in Alexandria, where the public high school, T. C. Williams, had an excellent academic reputation but also had a large number of underachieving students and was very crowded. She was about to enter the city's ninth-grade school Minnie Howard, which had 800 students, and each grade at the high school was at least that large.

Her parents and her sister, who was beginning graduate studies at American University, thought the ninth-grade school was acceptable. But, they said, Christin was a very bright student ready to start high school right now. Why slow her down?

The Alexandria school officials said Minnie Howard would have all the advanced courses that any ninth grade would have, but there just wasn't room for four grades in the old T. C. Williams building. That did not sway the Roaches, who wanted Christin to have the psychological and educational experience of interacting with older students and teachers of higher grades.

The easy transition that the Minnie Howard School was designed to provide seemed to the Roaches to be an unnecessary delay that might dilute the richness of a good high school.

So Roach's father was very excited to read about IB at Mount Vernon, three miles away. His daughter would have access to the AP program at T. C. Williams once she got there, but it looked to him like the IB was more rigorous. Their plan for Christin since elementary school was to expose her to the most challenging academic program possible, and IB seemed to be it. After more research, they were convinced, and bought a house a mile from the Mount Vernon High School campus just before the youngest Roach entered the ninth grade.

Calhoon's intake system was ready for her. She was given a detailed introduction to the pre-IB courses and the other hurdles she would face. Roach met Calhoon in her sunny little office down the hall from the principal, and reviewed the course options. They set up a tentative four-year plan, to be reviewed each year and perhaps adjusted as her interests evolved. Calhoon told Roach, as she told all IB applicants, about the hard work the program would demand, the care with which she should organize her extracurricular activities and study hours, and how well she would have to do on the exams to receive credit at college.

Roach was very clear about her motives. She had always wanted to take the most difficult classes. Her family had instilled in her the feeling that she could and should take them because she would do well in them. They would prepare her for the next step in her education. She was determined to earn the full IB diploma.

Her parents, having done their research on what this entailed, stepped back somewhat from their usual insistence that their daughter go for the maximum dose of whatever academic regimen she was taking. The thought occurred to them, as it had to many parents and teachers, that such a schedule might fry her circuits and leave her bitter and exhausted. They were concerned about how she would handle those subjects that she did not plan to pursue in college and in life—particularly math and the sciences.

So they occasionally reminded her, just to lower the temperature a bit, that if she decided not to be a full diploma candidate, or did not score high enough on the IB exams to get the diploma, it would not be the end of the world. Her abilities would not be in question. She was going to get into a good college. Any significant number of IB courses would help get her there and ensure her success there, with an IB diploma or not.

And then, just to make sure she realized she still had their confidence, they said that if she stuck with the diploma program, they would support her all the way.

Long after she graduated, Roach remembered the day at the end of her sophomore year that she absolutely decided to go for the IB diploma. The memory was attached to something else she did that day that people did not usually associate with IB. It was the day she ordered her class ring.

All of her friends were still saying they were going for the IB diploma, but she could tell a few were wavering. They had seen the frantic looks on the faces of some IB seniors in the last week before their extended essays were due. They began to realize how hard it would be to do that research project as well as pass very difficult exams in subjects that had been weak spots for them.

For Roach, the ultimate fear factors were science and mathematics. It was hard for her to put so much work into subjects in which she had a limited interest, but there was no escaping the fact she would have to do so if she wanted an IB diploma.

Ring selection time came for the class of 2001, and one of the options the ring company offered was the IB symbol for those who were sure they would get the diploma. Many of Roach's friends wanted the distinguished-looking emblem on their rings but were timid about ordering it without knowing if they would remain in the full IB or, as they put it, "go partial" and take just a few IB courses. Some of them were afraid that they would order their ring with the IB symbol and then fail to receive the diploma and be mocked forever, at least in their own minds, by this tangible reminder of their shortcomings.

Roach decided she would use this uncertainty to motivate herself. She ordered the gold class ring, with the IB emblem on one side and the National Honor Society emblem on the other. This, she said to herself, was a way to stay on track. She wore the ring almost every day of her junior and senior years, and whenever she felt like giving up, studied the IB symbol to remind herself that she was fully committed. She even wrote one of her college application essays about that decision, and how it seemed small and trivial, but had large and far-reaching consequences.

A Teacher Struggles to Make the Grade

Lured by the chance to become a better teacher at a more demanding school, Dan Coast was finishing his first year in IB Biology at Mount Vernon in the summer of 1998. It was clear to him he was in trouble.

Coast was an emotional man and a very energetic teacher. He had spent the year teaching three ninth-grade biology classes, plus one class of first-year IB Biology and one class of second-year IB Biology. He was beginning to wonder if he had made the right decision to leave his comfortable position as a popular science teacher in Charles County, Maryland, to step into the Fairfax County pressure cooker.

He stayed in his second floor Mount Vernon classroom until five or six o'clock every day, writing exhaustively detailed lesson plans so that he could use every precious minute in class to bring his students, and himself, up to the IB level. The problem was it did not seem to be working. The scores for his first group of seniors on the five-hour biology exam had just come back and they were not good.

The average score for those fifteen students was 3.8 on the 7-point examination. That was below 4, the minimum score for credit at most colleges, and below the international average score that year of 4.49. The feedback from the IB readers was brutal. They said he was not covering the syllabus efficiently. They said his students had no understanding of the Krebs cycle, an essential step in the release of energy from sugar and other organic molecules. He read the critique as saying, basically, that he was not doing a good job.

Coast's students had actually done better than the previous year's Mount Vernon IB Biology average of 3.36, when he was not yet at the school, but he didn't care about that. He felt himself tearing up as he finished his second reading of the paper. Was he really up to this? When Calhoon came by later to talk about the results, she could see how upset he was. She was easy on him, he thought. She just said the scores would have to improve. How was he going to do that?

Coast had attended high school in Fairfax County, at Hayfield High. His father had been in the army, and they lived in several places, until an accident in Vietnam took his father's life. His mother supported him and his older brother. He was a good student, on his way to being valedictorian at Hayfield, until his social life, expedited by his four-on-the-floor black Camaro, got in the way.

Still, he did his homework and did not give up on his studies. There was no IB program in Fairfax County then, but he had taken AP Biology and AP American History. He remembered his first test grade in the history course—only 4 out of 100 points. The night before the test there had been a crisis at home involving his brother, drugs, and the police. When he told the history teacher about it he got another chance, and did better. He got a 4 out of a possible 5 on the AP Biology examination, and was admitted to Virginia Tech.

He had wanted to be a teacher since sixth grade at Hayfield Elementary School, when Mr. Leganis had made him feel special by giving him accelerated math instruction. He graduated from college with a degree in biology in 1982, and after a few months working in a warehouse, got a teaching job in Charles County. By 1997 he had become a success at McDonough High School, teaching advanced biology, ecology, and regular biology, coaching softball, advising the ecology club and the environmental club, and having the satisfaction of hearing the students say they wanted to take his classes.

Joy McManus, chair of the Mount Vernon science department, called him to chat. She had taught at McDonough and liked Coast. He in turn saw Fairfax County, wealthier and higher performing than semirural Charles County, as a step up in the profession. Until that point he had been happy where he was and not thought about moving. But he had had a rough year—the superintendent had turned down a salary raise and a block scheduling plan he had worked on. He heard himself telling McManus that he might be interested in a change.

"Well, we really do need an IB Biology teacher," she said.

He drove over to inspect the Mount Vernon campus. It was certainly a convenient commute. He had a duplex in Alexandria, Virginia, a city popular with singles, including divorced people like Coast. It was a forty-five-minute drive to Charles County through heavy traffic on the Woodrow Wilson Bridge, the reverse direction from Bernie Glaze's commute. He could get to Mount Vernon from Alexandria in a much easier twenty-minute drive south on Route 1.

He was impressed, as he expected to be, with the equipment in Mount Vernon's classrooms. They all had computers and televisions and even a laser projector that allowed him to show molecules and internal organs and other biological representations in a simulated three dimensions. He also liked the greater ethnic diversity. McDonough High was 75 percent non-Hispanic white compared to Mount Vernon's 42 percent, and 36 percent of the students at the Fairfax County school were low income compared to only 9 percent at the Charles County school. The vibrancy and challenge of the IB program were also appealing.

When Calhoon asked what he could bring to the IB program, he talked about his success as a teacher, both with regular science students and with the advanced biology class that, although not as demanding as IB, showed that he could work at that level. When she asked what he considered his weaknesses, he admitted he would have to learn how to use the many electronic teaching aids at Mount Vernon that were new to him.

Calhoon and the rest of the administrators were pleased by his honesty, and his eagerness to become a better teacher. Tucker offered him the job.

When he was told that he was not far enough on the Fairfax salary steps to match his $45,000 annual salary in Charles

County, he wrote the personnel office a long letter and they bumped him up another $2,000 to match his old pay.

He enjoyed his week of training at the United Nations International School. He had an old friend who worked at UNIS. When she introduced him to the school's personnel director, the administrator tried to persuade Coast to take an opening he had. But Coast considered the Washington area his home, and came back to Mount Vernon anxious to get started.

As he had foreseen, it was not easy, and that became even more apparent as he analyzed the examination he would be preparing his students for.

The test had three parts, or what the IB people, in the European fashion, called "papers." Paper One lasted one hour and fifteen minutes and had forty multiple choice questions for the Higher Level, or two-year, version of IB Biology. They covered the entire range of the course.

When Coast arrived at Mount Vernon High in 1997, Paper Two consisted of just questions about experimental data, which in later years expanded to include short answer and short essay questions, with some choices, covering the entire course. The experimental questions were very new to Coast, and quite exciting. The students were given data charts, graphs, and other materials collected from a laboratory experiment, and then answered a series of short questions to show that they could analyze what they were seeing.

Paper Two was two hours and thirty minutes long, giving the student an opening block of three hours and forty-five minutes of test taking. They went home and came back the next day to take Paper Three, which took another one hour and thirty minutes.

Paper Three was a feast of choices from seven subject areas. Teachers were told to focus on any two of those seven in their courses, and their students would be tested just on those two. Coast had chosen his two strengths, evolution and ecology, and prepared his students for short-answer questions on both relevant experimental data and on related concepts.

As he reminded himself often, he had been working as an educator for fifteen years and had developed a reputation for excellence. But those good reviews from students and parents had much to do with his friendly teaching style and pleasant personality. He had never before been forced to work hard to achieve concrete standards of learning that would be expected of all his students. Never before had he had to prepare his students for a test that he did not write or score.

He had had lesson plans at McDonough, but no one assessed them and there was no way for anyone to know how well he had prepared his students, except for the few stars who took the SAT II biology achievement test. He had plenty of time after class at McDonough to coach and advise clubs, but he cut back on those activities at Mount Vernon. Instead he was in his classroom making plans to fill his ninety-minute block schedule classes, meeting every other day.

There was so much writing in IB Biology. To prepare for those essays in Paper Two, he was grading longer homework assignments than ever before. Each lesson plan had to match the IB standards, just as his lesson plans for his ninth-grade biology classes had to match the standards for the Virginia Commonwealth Standards of Learning exam, eventually a graduation requirement for all students.

And then there were the labs, many more of them than he had ever conducted in Charles County. The national standard for AP Biology classes was twelve to fifteen hours of labs, and in his most demanding class at McDonough, Advanced Biology, Coast did about ten hours.

That was not even close to the IB requirements. For a Higher Level course, the minimum was sixty hours of labs over two years. The laboratory data analysis questions on Papers Two and Three demanded it.

He did not like the textbook he had the first two years, and it took him a while to find one that was compatible to IB. He found that the juniors coming into his first-year IB Biology class, despite the fact that most had taken pre-IB science courses, still found the IB course a big adjustment. IB did not allow the teacher to lower the standard, as most teachers would do if faced with so many students who were not getting it. He had to bring them up to full speed. It was difficult at first, but he developed a trick that seemed to work.

Whenever he gave a lab the first quarter of the junior year course, he calibrated the grades and returned the students' lab reports with a special message. The labs were hard for them. They were no longer just memorizing terms and parroting the text book. They had to handle real materials that often did not behave the way they were supposed to, and they had little experience in describing what they were seeing.

Often he would give back a lab report with a D or an F on it. The student would visibly cringe, wondering if this was the end of his dreams of med school. Coast would immediately explain his unusual rules: "Some of you have gotten disappointing grades, I know. But I am not going to put those in the computer until you have a chance to rewrite what you have done. You need to rewrite it. You don't understand the standards yet and I don't expect you to understand the standards yet. I don't expect you to have mastered this. But this is what you have to do for mastery, and you better be there by the time you finish this course."

Their flaws were easy to predict. They would write a hypothesis that they could not support. They would not relate their procedures to their hypothesis. Their evaluation of the laboratory exercise would be too superficial. They would not take into account sources of errors and limitations in their experiments.

So they would rewrite, and sometimes rewrite again. If the first rewrite was an A or B, he put that in the computer. If it was a C or less, he had them rewrite it again. They were disappointed when they saw the low grades, but the shock was significantly eased by the happy thought that it would not count until they gave it another try. Coast did not want to chase them away from the course with those Ds and Fs when he knew they were capable of As and Bs. They just needed more time.

But it took him a while to become that confident of his method. When he saw the low IB scores at the end of his first year, he was tearful, and then determined to get better. Another year of late nights refining his lesson plans yielded no progress, in fact a drop to an average score of 3.42. The first year he could

at least entertain the thought that someone else had taught these
seniors their junior year, so maybe that teacher was partially at
fault. But in his second year the scores were of the students he
had had when they were juniors, and every year after he would
keep the same students both years. So whatever happened was his
fault, and no one else's.

30

Inside the IB Exams

The nature of the IB exams often came as a shock to American educators. Four- or five-hour tests taken over two days demanded a level of thought, analysis, concentration, and stamina not usually expected of American teenagers. The nature of the questions, the selection, and the scoring were also new to them.

The three-hour AP exams were also very demanding, but the IB exams had a little extra. Take, for instance, the AP and IB Biology examinations in May 2002.

Half of the AP Biology exam was multiple-choice questions. The other half was four free-response questions, one asking about continuity and change in the human genome, one seeking analysis of a chart of biorhythms of a mammal, and one asking about complexity of structure and function across the animal kingdom. The fourth question was about a laboratory experiment. It was the closest approximation to the lab questions found in Paper Two of the IB Biology exam. The fourth free-response question for AP Biology in 2002 was:

4. The following experiment was designed to test whether different concentration gradients affect the rate of diffusion. In this experiment, four solutions (0% NaCl, 1% NaCl, 5% NaCl, and 10% NaCl) were tested under identical conditions. Fifteen milliliters (mL) of 0% NaCl were put into a bag formed of dialysis tubing that is permeable to Na^+, Cl^-, and water. The same was done for each NaCl solution. Each bag was submerged in a separate beaker containing 300 mL of distilled water. The concen-

tration of NaCl in mg/L in the water outside each bag was measured at 40-second intervals. The results from the 5% bag are shown in the table below.

The table showed the concentrations of NaCl at zero, 40, 80, 120, and 160 seconds. Then the test taker was told to do the following:

(a) On the axes provided, graph the data for the 5% NaCl solution.

(b) Using the same set of axes, draw and label three additional lines representing the results that you would predict for the 0% NaCl, 1% NaCl, and 10% NaCl solutions. Explain your predictions.

(c) Farmlands located near coastal regions are being threatened by encroaching seawater seeping into the soil. In terms of water movement into or out of plant cells, explain why seawater could decrease crop production. Include a discussion of water potential in your answer.

Dan Coast's biology seniors at Mount Vernon sat down on May 9 to take the much longer four-and-a-half hour IB exam. The morning portion of the exam, called Paper One, included forty multiple choice questions for seventy-five minutes, similar to the ninety-minute multiple choice section of the AP exam. In the afternoon, however, when the students opened Paper Two, they found this lab question:

1. Metals such as zinc, nickel, and copper are toxic to most plants. However, some terrestrial plants can store quite a lot of these metal ions in their tissues. These plants are called hyperaccumulators and could be valuable in reducing the levels of such metal ions in the soil.

   Some species of Alyssum are known to be hyperaccumulators. Two of these Alyssum species were grown in nutrient solutions with different concentrations of nickel ions. As a control, each species was grown in nutrient solution which contained no nickel. The following chart shows the biomass production for each species.

The chart looked like a picket fence, with biomass production for each of two Alyssum species, lesbiacum and montanum, rising to different heights depending on the nickel concentration. The test taker was asked to:

(a) Identify the nickel concentration at which the biomass production is equal to the control in A. lesbiacum.
(b) Compare the effect of nickel concentration on the growth of both species of Alyssum.
(c) Suggest why a nutrient solution was used instead of soil.

Paper Two presented another graph showing the percentage of nickel in the dry biomass of the shoots and roots of the plants. It asked the test taker to:

(d) Calculate the change in the percentage of nickel in the dry biomass of A. lesbiacum roots when the nickel concentration is increased from 0.1 to 1.0 mmol dm^{-3}.
(e) Compare the percentage dry biomass of nickel in the roots and shoots between the two species.
(f) Suggest a reason for the difference in the percentage dry biomass of nickel in roots and shoots between A. montanum and A. lesbiacum.
(g) Predict, with an explanation, which species would be most useful in decontaminating soils containing high levels of nickel.

Another data chart appeared on the page, with this explanation: "Aquatic environments can be contaminated with pollutants, some of which are organic. An example of this occurred in the Willamette River near Portland, Oregon in the United States. The tissue concentration of polychlorinated biphenyls (PCB) was measured in three species of fish in two areas of the river. The data are given in parts per billion (ppb)."

Then the test taker was asked to:

(h) Calculate the mean concentration of PCB found in the tissue of the three species in each area.
Area 1:
Area 2:

Chapter 30

   (i) Compare the amounts of PCB found in Micropterus sp. and C. carpo [two of the fish species listed in the chart].

   (j) The concentration of dissolved PCB in the river is 0.01 ppb. Suggest a reason for the PCB concentration in the three species of fish found in the Willamette River.

The exam moved on to several shorter questions. The students took Paper Three the next morning.

Four days later on May 13, the Mount Vernon students taking Higher Level History of the Americas sat down for their Paper Two. It was a different exercise altogether, with a wide choice in several broad question areas. The highest scores would go to those who provided the most insights and best analysis. In the first section, they had ninety minutes to answer two questions, each from a different topic area. The questions in each topic, with the European spelling of some words, were:

Topic 1: Causes, practices and effects of war

  1. Compare and contrast the causes of the First and Second World Wars.

  2. Analyse the changes in the nature of warfare during the twentieth century.

  3. Why were there so many civil wars in the twentieth century?

  4. Examine the effects of war and the fear of war on the civilian population of two countries, each chosen from a different region.

  5. "The Korean War was a limited war, a civil war, and an episode in the Cold War." To what extent do you agree with each part of this assertion?

Topic 2: Nationalist and independence movements, decolonisation and challenges facing new states

  6. For what reasons, and with what justification, was there opposition to colonial rule in two countries, each chosen from a different region?

  7. Assess the origin and outcome of two wars of decolonisation.

8. In what ways, and for what reasons, have economic and social problems hindered the development of either Cuba or other areas of the Caribbean?

9. Examine the political problems faced by either one African or one Indian state in the second half of the twentieth century.

10. "New states have found it impossible to implement democracy." To what extent do you agree with this verdict?

Topic 3: The rise and rule of single-party states

11. Analyse conditions that led to single-party states during the twentieth century.

12. Compare and contrast the domestic policies of Hitler and Stalin.

13. In what ways, and for what reasons, did two rulers of single-party states, each chosen from a different region, fail to achieve their objectives?

14. Explain and examine the methods used by one of the following rulers of single-party states, to obtain and keep power: Lenin; Mao; Peron.

15. Assess the treatment of women and religious groups in two single-party states.

Topic 4: The establishment and work of international organisations

16. Account for the establishment of two international or two regional organisations.

17. Compare and contrast the social and economic policies of the League of Nations and the United Nations.

18. Analyse the political role and the impact of one of the following: the Arab League; the Commonwealth; the Organization of American States.

19. Assess the main successes and failures of one regional or international organisation during the second half of the twentieth century.

20. To what extent was the failure of any two international and/or regional organisations to achieve their objectives due to factors beyond their control?

Topic 5: The Cold War

21. In what ways, and for what reasons, did super-power rivalry dominate international politics between 1945 and 1961?
22. Analyse the role of Germany in the origin and development of the Cold War.
23. Explain and evaluate the impact of the Cold War on developing countries.
24. "A product of the Cold War, and a reason for the prolonging of Cold War tension." To what extent do you agree with this statement about the Vietnam War?
25. For what reasons, and with what effects, did social and cultural differences affect the origin and development of the Cold War?

Topic 6: The state and its relationship with religion and with minorities

26. Examine the relationship with the state of (a) one minority religion and (b) one majority religion.
27. Using examples to support your answer, assess the importance and extent of religion as a political factor since 1950.
28. In what ways, and for what reasons, has the position of racial and ethnic minorities deteriorated in two countries, each chosen from a different region?
29. Why have racial or ethnic minorities tried to preserve their cultures, and what problems have they faced in doing so?
30. To what extent, and for what reasons, did religious, racial, or ethnic persecution take place during the twentieth century?

Paper Three in the History of the Americas gave a similarly wide choice. The student had to pick three out of twenty-five questions, ranging from how well the Articles of Confederation addressed the grievances in the Declaration of Independence to the change in the relationship between Canada and Britain between 1900 and 1931 to the reasons for the U.S. intervention in Guatemala in 1954.

Nine days later on May 22 Mount Vernon's IB Computer Science students took Paper One, twenty questions of varying complexity that they had two hours to complete.

Question 1 was: "State which data type is best for storing a telephone number (e.g. 01623 440325) and give two reasons why."

Question 10 was: "State the function of the mantissa and exponent in the representation of a floating point number."

Question 16 was long and complicated, with five separate parts that asked the test taker to look at "the start of a trace table for the following algorithm" and state the function and purpose of certain lines.

Question 20 described five components that worked together in a typical operating system and asked four questions about their workings, including "Describe one advantage and one disadvantage of having a GUI as the user interface."

The exams would be packed up and sent to IB graders around the world. Each exam would be scored on a scale of 7 down to 1. Universities that acknowledged IB test results usually did not give credit for any exam that scored less than 4. A candidate who scored 4 on each of the six required exams would get a point total of 24, the minimum required for an IB diploma. Higher scores on some exams could balance out scores below 4 on other exams and still get the candidate the necessary 24 points.

It was different from anything else in American high schools, and new IB teachers in the United States would discover that it took getting used to.

IB in New Places

Much of the increased American interest in IB grew out of Nicol's introductory seminars and teacher training workshops. In 1978 he sent seminar notices to 6,600 North American public school boards and 1,500 private schools. The first nine seminars were not well attended, with only four people showing up in Boston. Houston, with the best attendance, drew only twenty-one participants. But it was a start.

Twenty-one of the thirty-nine schools that applied for IB programs in 1982 and 1983 did so only after first sending representatives to a seminar. Nicol said the twenty-six applications he received in June 1983 were "largely attributable to the schools wanting to send teachers to the September 1983 Teacher Training Workshops."

The IB North America director found that presentations at major teacher or administrator conferences worked even better. He held no seminars in Canada in 1980 because the joint meeting of the Canadian Association of School Administrators and the Canadian Education Association provided all the exposure he needed. The Canadians had nothing like the American AP program, and seemed even more eager for IB than their counterparts to the south.

The training workshops created good feeling by showing the program had well-organized support. AP did not provide much training for teachers, but IB did. At the workshops, prospective IB teachers met educators from all over the world. The first training workshops were held in 1978—two weekend meetings in

New York that drew 97 teachers from 26 schools. In 1982 there were 283 teachers from 54 schools and in 1984 there were 579 teachers from 125 schools, coming to workshops in Calgary, Chicago, New York, and Las Vegas.

The trainers were usually recruited from the faculties of some of the North America IB schools, such as UNIS and Francis Lewis and Pearson College. At first, IB North America paid the room and board for up to three teachers from each school and gave a travel grant of up to $150 each, depending on distance. But the organization's financial troubles put a stop to that, and attendance suffered.

In his 1982 progress report, Nicol summed up the early years:

IB schools in North America seem to have little in common except a consensual interest among teachers and administrators in the aims of the IB program. This is certainly true of the most recent group of admitted schools and is probably just as true for those who have joined in past years. At the risk of over-generalization, it is the case that some schools serve rural areas, others small municipalities in out of the way places, and a number of them urban centers or the surrounding suburbs of major metropolitan areas. Their eleventh- and twelfth-grade enrollments range from less than 100 to more than 600. Their communities range from those that are affluent to those with sizable portions of their populations below or near the poverty level.

Some have had long years of experience with challenging academic programs like AP and others have not. Still others, like the new IB school in New Mexico, The Armand Hammer United World College of the American West, with all its students in the IB program, are part of independent school committees that have had previous experience and exposure to the IB program. Some IB schools have achieved national recognition, but many are unknown outside their immediate vicinity. Almost all IB schools have had honor courses in the upper grades in one guise or another, but only 62 percent of those in the United States authorized in 1981-2 had been offering one or more College Board Advanced Placement examinations.

Some of the new IB schools in the United States were very different from the international schools that had spawned the program. In 1978, as part of a plan to desegregate the Milwaukee school system by creating a series of challenging magnet schools, Rufus King High School was designated an academic high school for college-bound students, with the new IB program as its principal attraction. Until IB was introduced, Rufus King students had nearly all been African American teenagers from the neighborhood. After students throughout the city were invited to enroll there for IB, the demographics changed significantly. In five years, according to a *St. Petersburg Times* story, the school was no longer predominantly black, but 55 percent non-Hispanic white. Still, nearly 24 percent of the students in the IB program were African American, one of the highest percentages of blacks at any IB program in the country, or the world for that matter.

Ninety-eight percent of the IB students at Rufus King were going to college. Its once poor disciplinary record had become one of the best in the city. Only five students had taken IB exams in 1979, but by 1984 that number was eighty-six, with seven getting the full diploma.

Peterson loved hearing about IB engaging minority students. In the early 1980s a guidance counselor at Harlingen High School in Harlingen, Texas, walked into Peterson's office after reading about IB in a magazine during a flight to London. "Half my kids are Mexican Americans," the man told Peterson, "and some of them are very bright, particularly in math. They ought to be getting into the best colleges, but what admissions officer is going to pay much attention to a transcript or diploma from a small town they've never heard of deep in the heart of Texas? So I want your program for them."

By 1984 Harlington High had twenty-two students taking IB tests, including two candidates for the diploma. One Harlingen IB student had gotten a scholarship at Caltech. The University of Texas at Austin was coming to see what other Harlingen students it could recruit.

IB or Not IB

Emmet Rosenfeld had non-IB as well as IB English classes. The contrasts between them revealed much about the difference between IB and the rest of American high school education.

There was no prescribed reading list for Rosenfeld's regular classes, for instance. Sometimes he would choose the books. Sometimes students would. He knew that many eleventh-grade teachers required certain works of American literature, like Arthur Miller's play *The Crucible*. Rosenfeld showed a video of the play, and read some passages, but he used the spinning plates system with them too. Everyone might have a different book to read, and he would keep them all engaged by asking them to discuss and write about themes and characterizations and writing devices.

If he thought the regular students were picking books beneath their grade level, he would nudge them upward. Yet once he gave them the choice, they surprised him. They would often pick very good books.

The laziest of the group would pick Steinbeck's *Of Mice and Men*, because they had already read it in the ninth grade, but Rosenfeld did not mind that so much. Rereading books had advantages. Once they realized that he was serious about regular reading, and that they would have to write about what they had read, the threat of boredom persuaded many clever slackers to pick something they had not seen before.

Rosenfeld also let the regular students have some say in how many books they would read. "I have a very simple requirement for this class," he said. "I want you to read more books than you have ever read before in your life."

This usually brought a complaint: "Huh? I don't like to read." But once they started on something that appealed to them it was hard to stop. The IB class was doing at least eight books and plays, but the regular class did not look so bad by comparison. Some non-IB students would read twelve to fifteen books. Some would only read four or five. In many regular classes, Rosenfeld knew, some students could not bring themselves to read any of the required books. He thought reading anything was better than reading nothing, and made sure they had a choice.

He would give them at least half of the ninety-minute class period to do the reading. Once they got into it, he might expand that time if there was enough demand. Some students fell asleep during the reading period, but most applied themselves to their books. His rule was the students had to have their journals open beside their books so that they would be ready to make an observation on something that interested them.

He had a format they had to follow for their journal entries, or what he called their reader responses. With the IB kids, he could have them focus on ideas. With the regular students, he first had to ask them to look for difficult vocabulary. They wrote down in their journals words they did not understand, and later looked them up in their dictionaries, drawing pictures in their journals as a mnemonic device to implant the meanings in their brains. He had to be careful to check the regular students' reader responses to make sure they were done completely. He could count on all but a few of the IB students to do their homework, but the regular kids needed reminding.

In IB classes Rosenfeld reserved less time for reading and doing homework, and more time for teaching. He had many more group activities in IB, such as the fish bowls or the color coding or a favorite of his called The Long Sentence. In order to teach the proper use of the colon and the semicolon, he would have each group create a lengthy list of statements about the books they were reading and then connect everything with the proper punctuation.

But there were approaches he could take with both IB and regular classes. He assigned projects in the same way. The students would make proposals and if he approved them they would start work. Many of them were PowerPoint presentations, but some were old-fashioned term papers.

It was important to give them a choice, Rosenfeld thought, particularly in the regular class. He said, "Okay, you can write a literary analysis or you can do a pastiche," IB's term for writing in the style of the author being read and including a statement of intent in which they explained exactly how they imitated the author.

He had the same policy for exams and tests in both IB and regular classes. He never gave them. He would have exercises that prepared the IB students for their big IB test in May, but there would never be a Mr. Rosenfeld test they had to pass.

Instead, he assessed them by their work, the portfolio method of grading. The quarter grade would be based on their daily journals and class work. Whatever assignment they had they always added to the journal. It might be note-taking, it might be brainstorming, it might be free writing, or it might be writing to a prompt, a question, as the IB students would have to do in the IB test. They were told to date each journal entry and keep an orderly table of contents. Each quarter he would collect the journals and grade them.

They also graded their own journals with a self-evaluation checklist for each assignment. A student would, for instance, mark that he had written down five attributes of the short story he was reading and had made a story diagram, but would not mark the part of the check list that asked if he had taken notes on the story, because they had not done that. Rosenfeld would check to make sure they had graded themselves accurately.

The IB students were required to make notes in their books, something the regular students did not have to do. Annotating was a big part of IB, because the idea was to be close to the text. That slowed down some students. Roland would keep up his notations but his friend Daniel would fall far behind.

As IB grew at Mount Vernon, the ratio of regular to IB classes changed. By 2003, for eleventh-grade English, there were six classes of IB to eight classes of regular, although the IB classes were smaller—about twenty students each—while the regular classes were closer to thirty students. Rosenfeld knew some students in his regular classes could handle IB, but he didn't push them to switch. They had other priorities. Many of them took IB in some subjects, but either did not like English classes or did not want the added stress of the full diploma program.

One of Rosenfeld's regular students won a writing award from the National Council of Teachers of English. The boy had coasted in school, and gotten Bs from Rosenfeld. He made it clear that if the teacher had dared ask him why he wasn't taking IB English, he would have said, "Because I don't want to." About a third of the students in Rosenfeld's regular classes were better than the worst students in his IB classes. They learned something in English, but at their own pace.

Rosenfeld tried to match his IB grading policy to the district's policies, and his own need to motivate students. He gave few As, but was generous with Bs. The usual class of twenty IB students might see two or three As, ten or eleven Bs, three or four Cs, and one or two Ds or Fs. Cs were for students like Daniel who stuck it out, did most of the work, but were not very good at it. In his regular classes Rosenfeld gave many more Cs than he did in his IB classes.

Peterson Looks Back

In July 1977 Peterson retired as director general, turning the title over to Renaud in Geneva who was already in charge of the day-to-day operation of the IBO. That brought the director general back to the head office of the organization in Geneva, with other IBO offices including a separate examinations service in the United Kingdom and emerging regional offices in Buenos Aires, Singapore, and London. IB North America was an independent operator in legal and financial terms, but also acted as a regional office.

In 1983, Renaud retired and Roger Peel, a professor of foreign languages at Yale and Middlebury, born and raised in England, became director general.

In his memoir, Peterson said his greatest IB satisfaction, as a professor of education interested in improving schools, was the success of the TOK course, as well as the extended essay and the CAS requirement. Of TOK, he said, "Since most schools belonged to the anglophone tradition, to which the inclusion of anything that appeared to be 'philosophy' was unfamiliar, we learned much in the development of the Theory of Knowledge course from our French collaborators, who saw clearly that the nature of the course was not a history of ideas, nor a course in epistemology, nor one in symbolic logic, and yet drew to some extent on all three."

In the early days of the extended essay, Peterson noted, students were warned not to try topics that were too broad, like Chinese foreign policy in the twentieth century, or for which material was not available. It also took time for students to realize that they would indeed be punished if their essays were longer than 4,000 words. R. S. Bourne's 1977 survey of essay topics said there were too many that took a historical figure and "slung a pseudo-historical study" around him or her. Out of a sample of eighty-one essays, Bourne found fifteen on Hitler and Nazism, sixteen on Russian revolutionaries, and eleven on other famous dictators. There was also a strong tendency to write about the problems of racial minorities from a very personal perspective.

But there were also serious pieces of local history, such as one paper called "Agricultural and Food Marketing Systems of Sri Lanka," and some high quality scientific reports based on individual fieldwork and experiments.

The public service requirement produced a stream of queries to Peterson about what would suffice. When someone asked if playing soccer would qualify, Peterson said no, but organizing a youth soccer team would. Going to an art gallery would not be enough unless it was part of a regular club activity, he said. He worried that the requirement might be diluted, but thought it was worth pursuing.

Before his death in 1989 he noted with satisfaction the growth of IB in public schools in the United States and the Nordic countries. IBO officials who knew Peterson said he would have been particularly pleased to see that by 2004, 55 percent of all students taking IB diploma examinations around the world would be from public schools that charged no tuition fees, with the majority of such IB schools being in the United States and Canada.

IB was reaching beyond the favored children of international diplomats and businessmen it had started with, and advancing Peterson's desire, influenced by his memories of World War II, that IB's curriculum make the world a bit smaller. "Unless the next generation of the young are brought up in such a way as to stimulate, liberate, and educate their natural propensity to make friends across frontiers—national, racial and cultural," he said at the end of his memoir, "we, the educators, are failing in our responsibility to our children."

34

Andrew Johnson, Bill Clinton, and Christin Roach

The fun parts of IB for Christin Roach were English and Theory of Knowledge. The tough parts were chemistry and math. Sometimes TOK annoyed her when the teacher asked questions that seemed beside the point, like "How do you know you know?" The query either had no answer or a dozen different answers, depending on the circumstances.

But as she approached the IB exams, and then college, she began to see the relevance of this kind of inquiry. In her philosophy and political science courses at Boston University, she would come to realize that there were no absolute answers to most important questions. Points of view differed and it was hard to fix on one aspect of a cause-and-effect relationship without any of the others.

At Mount Vernon she kept at her IB studies, and began to enjoy the connections between disciplines. There were many late nights, but her parents gave her a new five-CD stereo system that kept her energy up. Toward the end she wondered how she had ever had a doubt about her chances of getting the diploma.

She even found, somewhat to her surprise, that she enjoyed the required 150 hours of community service. She began volunteering at Mount Vernon Hospital on Friday nights, along with a number of other IB students. She liked working with her classmates. The senior volunteers, retirees in the community, seemed delighted to have the teenagers around. It turned out to be one of the best experiences of her high school years. She did far more than 150 hours and won an award as best junior volunteer. She began to see how such a commitment could enrich her life, just as IB was strengthening her studies. She would remain in contact with one of the adult volunteers long after high school.

But even with such a schedule, she still had some free time. She worked on the yearbook and was coeditor of the school's art and literary magazine. She rarely missed the television drama *ER*, even with heavy Thursday night homework. On the weekends, she went out with her friends for dinner and a movie, and a stop of Baskin-Robbins for some discount ice cream, since one member of her group worked there. Toward the end of her high school years she also worked at the Gap store in the Pentagon City Mall every Friday and Saturday.

The biggest challenge for her, as it was for most IB students, was the extended essay. Her topic was ripped from the headlines, as might be expected of a future journalism major. Her title was "The Unconstitutional Presidential Impeachments of Andrew Johnson and Bill Clinton." They were not only the only presidents to be impeached, but in both cases, she argued, the bill of impeachment had been brought improperly. She examined the origins of the Tenure of Office Act that Johnson had allegedly violated, and found contemporary opinions of its dubious constitutionality. In the Clinton case, she looked at the legal definition of high crimes and misdemeanors, and examined whether the president's lies to the public and before a judge reached that level of severity based on the subject matter of the testimony.

She loved the chance to explore a contemporary issue so deeply, although she worried she did not have enough time to give it the attention it deserved. She had to write papers for some of her six IB courses that senior year, and an insightful essay of 4,000 words would have been hard to bring off even if it were the only assignment she had.

Calhoon realized the pressures on Roach and the other seniors, and tried to schedule after-school meetings with them to make sure they were staying on track. She would offer advice on how best to use their time. Often these busy students did not show up, and so she tracked them down, one by one, to make sure they were keeping up.

The IB coordinator's persistence annoyed some of Roach's friends. They said Calhoon was just doing it to increase her numbers and make herself look good. But Roach, who had watched Calhoon closely for four years, was convinced that she was impelled by a desire to keep young people from wasting a prime opportunity, at a moment in their lives when they had only TV and sports and parties, not jobs and children, to keep them from getting an education.

Calhoon talked about potential. It was a broken record with her, but Roach shared the teacher's view that she should push herself to the limit. All of her friends had the ability to do the work, but some didn't see the benefit of taking harder classes when they could get the same grades, and in many cases better grades, in regular classes and still get into college.

Roach graduated from Mount Vernon in 2001 and spent the summer getting ready to study journalism at Boston University. The IB scores came, as they always did, as an anticlimax, long after the excitement of college acceptances and prom dresses and marching across the stage in cap and gown. There wasn't even a mysterious letter from Cardiff to rip open. Like the other IB graduates, Roach just went online when the scores were due, used her PIN number, and examined the numbers. She satisfied all of her requirements and received the full IB diploma.

That meant she arrived on the BU campus with twenty-four credits, eight credits each for English, French, and history. That was a semester and a half of college work, opening the way for her to enroll in a dual degree program, the Boston University Collaborative Degree Program, or BUCOP, in journalism and political science.

That was a big deal for Roach. The two majors were each in a different school in the university, which usually meant a student taking both would have to stay more than four years to get all the required courses fulfilled. But the IB credits solved the problem. She also found her experience at Mount Vernon kept her in good shape in those courses she did not like much, but had to take. And like most IB students, she found the heavy workload of a college freshman very similar to what she had had in high school.

35

Signs of Success

For Bud Spillane, the Fairfax County school superintendent, the first signs of success for IB at Mount Vernon High School came from, of all places, the Thomas Jefferson High School for Science and Technology. Spillane began to hear complaints about great teachers like Bernie Glaze abandoning his best high school to teach IB.

He heard that the new IB teachers loved the IB training. AP retained its prestige in the county, but AP teachers had no training requirement, and often did not get any special preparation. The certification for AP was often nothing more than a telephone call from a department chair that said, hey, teach this course. I am the department chair, so you are now an AP teacher. For IB to distinguish itself as a step above AP made Spillane very happy. The competition would help both programs, he thought.

Spillane could see that the reputations of the two new IB schools were getting a boost. Even better, jealous educators in some of the more affluent schools said they also wanted IB. They were saying that they needed something to demonstrate their academic rigor. Spillane thought to himself that if he had planned it that way, it could not have worked out better.

By the time Spillane retired in 1997 to take up a job supervising U.S.-supported overseas schools, Fairfax was on its way to putting IB in eight of its twenty-three academic high schools. Woodson High would eventually reject IB and go back to AP. Spillane thought it had been a mistake ever to introduce the program to a school whose faculty had not accepted it. But the overall change in approach had been a success. IB had been institutionalized, and no future superintendent would be able to dump it without a terrible ruckus.

Spillane was not so happy about attempts to introduce the IB Middle Years Program and Primary Years Program. He thought the county's curriculum in lower grades was already strong enough to prepare students for IB, without paying an extra fee for MYP or PYP. But that was for the schools and the new superintendent, the very pro-IB Daniel Domenech, to decide.

In his new job, Spillane encountered the International Baccalaureate much more frequently than he had as Fairfax superintendent. The international schools that he supervised in his job often used IB, and he would encounter many Americans living abroad who had doubts about subjecting their children to so much work.

"My kid has no chance for a social life," one parent complained.

Spillane, recounting the IB success of disadvantaged students at Stuart and Mount Vernon, recommended they give it a try. And to those who worried that IB focused too much on Europe and the rest of the world, and lacked an American focus, Spillane suggested they look at where the United States was in the world in the twenty-first century. "If we are becoming a global society," he said, "what is wrong with an international diploma? American education is already more international than most people believe. There is nothing purely American about our schools, and if you go to some of the international schools you don't see much of a difference. We are all doing the same kind of thing."

"If your children don't like IB, that's not the end of life. There are other programs. But they can at least say they tried it."

Amundson, the school board member who had gotten the money for IB at Mount Vernon, had her own suburban politician's measuring stick for what was working and what was not. The defining moment for her came about three years after IB began at Mount Vernon. She was at a neighborhood party, making the political rounds as usual, when she overheard a mother talking to other parents about the local schools.

Some of their children had gotten into private schools. Some were applying to Jefferson. And this mother had her own good news to share: "My daughter has been admitted to that very good IB program at Mount Vernon," she said.

There were no snorts of derision, no questions about whether that school was safe or the best place to learn. This group of parents accepted the notion that IB was among the many fine choices available to college-conscious Fairfax parents.

Hot damn, Amundson said to herself. She would later be elected to the Virginia House of Delegates and have other triumphs, but she told people that getting IB into Mount Vernon High was one of the things in her life of which she was most proud.

The Comeback Teacher

Very gradually, Dan Coast felt his IB Biology teaching getting better. He knew that if his students gained confidence in him, he was halfway to his goal of a class where everyone had a passing score. More of them were dropping by after school, making small talk, asking for extra help. He had succeeded in getting them to appreciate the higher standard they had to meet, and the time they had to devote to meet it.

He had grown accustomed to the laser disk, which allowed him to animate a biological process and liberate his students from the dense language of the textbook. He could freeze the image on the screen, ask the students if they understood it, move forward a bit, ask them to predict what would happen next, and keep that rolling. There were three television screens in his room—he never got over the technological riches of Fairfax County—and two of them were hooked up to the laser disk.

Homework varied. Some days he might give an hour's worth, other days less. He knew that most of his students were going for the IB diploma. IB Biology was one those courses that IB dabblers tended to avoid. He knew they were also getting much homework in their other IB classes, so he tried to be reasonable. His ninth-grade biology classes had twenty-six or twenty-seven students. His IB classes averaged about twenty. As he got better, he noticed almost all of the IB students were sticking with the class. In seven years only two dropped his course, and not because they were not understanding it, but because of conflicts with other things they wanted to do.

By 2003, his senior class had reached the average score of 4, 4.08 to be exact. Every day was still hard. The first-year IB Biology course was still a struggle. Every year he had to frighten the newbies with those Ds and Fs on their labs. But the second year class, the seniors, was a dream.

The school called that course IB Bio 2, and it had become, he realized, the most rewarding teaching experience of his life. Teachers like him were full of concepts and insights they ached to share with students, but they could rarely find that level of appreciation among teenagers. In IB Bio 2, he had achieved the fantasy—a group of students who knew what he was talking about and became as excited by a surprising quirk of nature as he was.

Each fall he sat down with his seniors in room A219 and felt almost like a college professor surrounded by very engaged graduate students. He had always drilled into his ninth graders this mantra: Take responsibility for your own education. These seniors did not have to be told that. They were doing it without his asking.

The labs went smoothly. The lab books came back with a professional look. They were designing the lab, writing the hypothesis, supporting the hypothesis, designing the materials and procedures, limiting the variables and analyzing the work. One of his seniors even did her extended essay in biology, a rare occurrence since the social science topics were usually more popular, and easier to bring off. An avid horsewoman, she had heard about a virus going around the stables of Northern Virginia, something relatively unknown in veterinary circles, and made it her subject.

On one of those days when he was feeling particularly good about the improvement in his teaching, Coast spoke up when Calhoon dropped by to give him some paperwork. "Betsy, as I have sat up here these last few years and gone through this IB program, and talked to some of the other teachers, I have to say I really like it. It has been a great move for me professionally," he said.

She thanked him, and that encouraged him to go on: "So if you ever think about retiring, throw my name in the hat."

She smiled and said she would remember. Three years later she approached him after school and asked if he was still interested in taking over. She and Chuck had their eye on the Beaufort, South Carolina, area, a land of beautiful marshes and a low cost of living, with lots of retired military, some of them old friends. Calhoon was going to be sixty. She thought it was time to let someone else steer young people into the wonders of research and analysis.

Coast said yes, right away. The next year he worked a couple of periods as Calhoon's administrative intern, learning the intricacies of working with both students and teachers, some of them under the same kind of stress he remembered so well. In August of 2003, Calhoon and her husband drove south, and Coast became the IB coordinator.

And on September 27 that year, at age forty-three, he became a father, as his wife Beth, a teacher he had met at McDonough, gave birth to Sam and Eliza, twins who made, as far as he was concerned, a very good year complete.

Making It Harder to Get IB

After Cliff Sjogren at the University of Michigan distributed his glowing letter about IB, Nicol persuaded him to join the IB North America board. He and Carus were the only two members from outside of New York and New England. By that point the board had nearly thirty people—part of a deliberate effort to involve as many influential persons as possible. They struggled with issues of diploma program expansion, workshops, and college recognition.

But the biggest problem was attrition. Some schools that had adopted IB were either dropping it or letting it die the typical slow death of inattention and underfunding whenever a principal or superintendent lost interest. Many schools, like love-struck teenagers, had chosen IB in the excitement of finding something new and challenging, then discovered the program required far more attention, energy, and money than they were willing to provide.

By the mid-1980s, 45 percent of schools that had at some time adopted IB in the United States were no longer active participants. A 1986 study by the IB North America board said the problem was inadequate preparation. The board decided to do something about it.

Henceforth schools that wanted to join IB had to undergo staff training, complete a comprehensive self-study, submit a formal application, and schedule a two-day visit to the school by a three-person team of IB delegates before their application was complete. The process usually took two to three years, but it produced dramatic results. The attrition rate for IB schools declined to 4 percent.

Nancy Weller succeeded Gil Nicol as regional director in 1986. The New York office was still small. When Paul Campbell, the future head of outreach, joined in 1988, there were only four staffers and IB was still almost unknown in the country, despite the growth in schools. "I used to joke that I think I got the job because I spelled the word baccalaureate correctly," Campbell said.

But as new schools adopted IB, they began to communicate directly with each other, bypassing the New York office. Regional networks were born without any direction from headquarters. Schools in one part of the country or another would see the advantages of keeping in touch with each other, sharing tips, and cooperating on training. Weller only tolerated the natural evolution of what came to be called sub-regional associations, but Campbell and Weller's successor, Bradley Richardson, encouraged them. By 2004 there were nearly two dozen such regional groups in the United States.

In 1992 Weller launched a three-times-a-year magazine, *IB World*, and began a joint publishing venture with the *Concord Review*, a referreed history periodical for high school student work, to present the best IB history extended essays.

The IB North America board created a five-year review of progress of participating schools. The growing system of school inspections and training sessions relied heavily on educators in IB schools volunteering their time, with only their expenses paid to travel to school districts where they would have to review new schools or check out old ones.

When Weller became director of communication for IB in Geneva in 1994, she was succeeded by the deputy regional director, Richardson, who before IB had worked at several colleges, creating and running remedial programs for freshmen. North America added its first regional manager for the Middle Years Program in 1994 and the first MYP teacher training workshops the next year in Denver and Montezuma, New Mexico. In 1995 Minnesota and Texas joined Florida in creating programs that reimbursed public schools for their IB training and test fee expenses. California and Colorado followed, and by 2004 eleven other states and the District of Columbia funded IB to the extent of subsidizing low-income student's test fees.

By the end of 1997, the growth of schools in the United States had put a severe strain on IB's New York office. The next year it moved from the twentieth floor of 200 Madison to more spacious quarters on the twenty-third floor, and the staff was increased to twenty full-time employees. It moved again in 2000 to even larger premises across town at 475 Riverside Drive.

Richardson oversaw the creation of a research unit to gather data from IB schools that could be used to assess their impact on learning. He organized an effort to find more ways to attract low income and minority students into IB, and to increase awareness of its distinct qualities, rather than continually describe it as a smaller, European-originated version of AP.

"People tend to say, 'Oh, it's like AP,' and that's fine," he said. "But we have ridden on those coattails to great heights, and we need to provide a more sophisticated understanding of what the IB diploma is all about."

Richardson said he also worried, as the New York office grew to thirty-two staffers in 2004, that it might become, if he was not careful, a traditionally stiff bureaucracy that defended itself rather than looked for ways to change and grow.

Despite the program's academic and financial success worldwide, the disagreements between the New York and European offices did not entirely disappear. The North American program, the only one to be adopted readily by growing numbers of state-funded schools, seemed destined to have more students than the rest of the IB programs combined, and fairly soon. That caused concern in Europe, but the two sides found ways to compromise. The American and British Commonwealth programs, for instance, resolved their old dispute over spelling—the IBO insisted on consistency. The British agreed to spell organization the American way, with a z rather than an s, and the Americans agreed to the British spelling of programme, with a silent "me" at the end.

Among testimonials to the program in the United States was one from Marilee Jones, director of undergraduate admission at the Massachusetts Institute of Technology. She called IB the "best high school prep curriculum an American school can offer." But the staff members in New York City reminded themselves repeatedly that rapid growth was a threat to quality and to future growth, and they encountered new roadblocks and annoyances that proved them right.

Why Nazis Are Like Marxists

Allen Rushing's classroom, A105, was perched on a corner of the white, spotless corridor of the Mount Vernon High School social studies wing. The school had grown in stages, fanning out over its large suburban campus, and this was one of the newer additions. The social studies wing had white-painted cinderblock walls with a maroon baseboard and halls wide enough to handle the usual between-classes rush.

Rushing had come to Mount Vernon after retiring from Stanton College Preparatory High School in Jacksonville, Florida, one of the premier IB and AP public schools in the country. He had liked the idea of living in D.C., with its historical and cultural attractions. As a history teacher it was his kind of place. When he heard about the job at Mount Vernon, it seemed to suit him. Like Mount Vernon, Stanton College Prep had also had a large contingent of minority students, and had made a national reputation for getting them into IB and AP courses in great numbers. Betsy Calhoon was delighted to get his application, for he was the first experienced IB teacher Mount Vernon had ever had a chance to hire.

In February 2004, twenty-two seniors were stuffed into his small classroom preparing for the IB Twentieth-Century History exam. The topic of the day was fascism in Germany, and the students were the usual mix: eleven boys and eleven girls, including three African Americans and three Hispanics.

"Let's get quiet please and see if we have any announcements," he said. It was the post-lunch period, reserved for loudspeaker bulletins. As arrangements for science fairs and buses for the freshman girls' basketball teams crackled out of the speakers in the ceiling, the seniors chatted among themselves, convinced by long experience that the news would be of no interest to them.

The announcements ended. "All right, let's get quiet," Rushing said again. He snapped on an overhead projector that showed an outline of the points he was going to make in this class period. "Let's take out a clean sheet of paper to take notes," he said.

As he talked, he slowly moved the outline across the screen, so that even the most distracted or somnolent student could copy down his points and not miss the basics. And it kept the students in context, for they could see how one point related to the next.

"What we are going to look at today are various aspects of National Socialism," he said. "We will see which aspects of Mr. Mussolini's definition actually appear in National Socialism." Some European philosophers had adopted national racism as a guiding principal of the state, and the Nazis picked that up. "This was a state of pure German people," he said, "but you need to realize what has been happening. What has been happening to races in Europe since the collapse of the Roman empire?"

"Interbreeding?" suggested one boy.

"Right," said Rushing. He would ask questions throughout the period, and try to show the contradictions revealed by critical thinking of the material before them. He wanted them to step back from the material and see the flaws and dissonances, in hopes of encouraging the same kind of analysis throughout the course. "Consequently it is very difficult to tell what would be considered a pure anything in Europe," he said. "But what you see in National Socialism is that they never allow facts, historical facts, to get in their way."

"This would be *Ein Volk, Ein Reich*"—he apologized for his accent to a German-speaking student—"One people, one country. There is going to be one single group of people. This would mean the exclusion of Jews, Gypsies, and the sick or infirm."

He led them through the list of territories outside the reduced, post–World War I Germany that had large numbers of ethnic Germans—Alsace Lorraine, Sudentenland, Danzig. "Because of immigration there were pockets of German people throughout Europe," he said. "That means a significant slice of territory, extending into modern . . . what?"

"Russia," someone said.

He began to explore the bizarre inconsistencies of Nazi doctrine as the party moved from the fringes of German politics in the 1920s into power in the 1930s. This was the kind of analysis that readers of IB papers and exams looked for. The students taking an IB exam would not be asked just to write down the facts they remembered, but contrast them with other facts and make points that helped explain why history took strange turns.

"In Nazi propaganda you have the peasant patronized as the ideal of National Socialist values," he said.

"What was the Russian element that saw the peasants as the basis of the revolution?" he asked. One student remembered— the Social Revolutionaries. "And what was the paradox with that?" he asked.

One tall boy, sitting at the left of the classroom, thought he had the answer: "He is going to need industry to start the war."

Rushing smiled and nodded. "Also, the industrial society provided Hitler and the National Socialists with money, so they are going to have to adjust," he said. "The industrial segment is the heaviest backer of Nazism, because they don't want the Communists. They have the most to lose."

Rushing was getting close to his main point. "The Nazis saw a classless society in the future of peasants and small tradesmen. Those were the two groups that they were mostly focusing on. This was in their early days, but that is very close to what?"

Several students responded: "Communism!"

"Right," Rushing said. "Marxism."

He moved on, pushing his projected outline down a few points. "Of course their thinking grows out of ethnic nationalism in the concept of racial superiority. Where does the term Aryan first appear in history?"

One boy knew: "India."

"Exactly," Rushing said, "and that is not the group that Hitler is talking about. What is the irony there?"

A girl suggested, "He doesn't look like that?"

"Right. He does not exemplify the ideal he is talking about."

He turned to the Slavs. "The National Socialists said those people were destined to be the slaves. The idea was that the state was to create a super race, and the purpose of the state was to make sure there was no mixing of these races. That is anti-miscenegation.

"But keep in mind that in the early 1970s an anti-miscegenation law still existed in Virginia. National Socialism also discussed the issue of sterilization. Has that ever popped up in American history?"

"Yes," said some students.

"With what group?"

"The mentally retarded," one boy said.

"Exactly."

Finally, they reached anti-Semitism. Rushing was careful to put the concept in context, something the IB examiners would watch for. "First thing, I always want to stress, anti-Semitism has had an extremely long history in Europe." He noted the origin of the word "ghetto" as a walled enclosure for Jews in Italy in the thirteenth century.

He reviewed some of their reading on Hitler—that he had been rejected by an art school in Austria and blamed the Jewish scholars at the school, that many Jews held prominent positions in Austria, that Marx's family had been Jews until his father converted to Lutherism to improve his financial standing, that Jews were influential in the Social Democratic Party, which many Germans blamed for losing World War I.

The bell rang. The students copied down the last parts of the outline, and filed out. They had several hours of homework ahead of them.

A New Principal Wants
More IB

Cathy Crocker, a former math teacher at Thomas Jefferson, arrived at Mount Vernon in 1997. She had just earned her doctorate in education—her thesis on interdisciplinary courses fit well with IB. She yearned to get back to working with students. She was assistant principal at Mount Vernon for a while, a job she had also held at Jefferson. When Calanthia Tucker was promoted to district headquarters in 1999, Crocker became principal.

She and Calhoon agreed precisely on what to do with the IB program. It had been widely recognized as a success, but that was not enough. They wanted more students participating, and they wanted more students from minority families and families where the parents had not attended college.

Crocker endorsed a tough love approach. Not only were counselors and teachers urged to encourage seemingly capable students to sign up for IB, but Crocker had her counseling staff begin to examine the scores on the eighth-grade Virginia Standards of Learning (SOL) tests for every child enrolling in Mount Vernon's ninth grade. If they found anyone who had scored more than 450 of a possible 600 points on the SOL in any subject, they would check to see if that student was signed up for the pre-IB course in that subject.

And if they weren't, the counselor would, as Crocker instructed, put them in that course without bothering to ask them first.

A letter would go to the parents, of course, telling them this had been done. It gave them the option of taking their child out of the pre-IB course if they wished. But during Crocker's first five years at Mount Vernon, only one parent did so.

Crocker explained why she adopted such an aggressive policy: "There is a tentativeness about kids coming into high school. They say, 'I don't know if I can do this or not,' so we have to say, 'We think you can.'"

Crocker had grown up in Dunkirk, New York, on Lake Erie near Buffalo. Her father had been the janitor at Dunkirk High School, where she was the valedictorian in 1970. She was a very active and outgoing student who already knew she wanted to be a math teacher. After graduating from Rensselaer Polytechnic Institute in 1974, she came to Fairfax County where her aunt, Mary Gibbons, was a math teacher at Woodson High, and got a job at McLean High.

She taught in other schools before she went to Jefferson when it opened in 1985 as a magnet school for the highest-scoring students in the area. She taught AP Calculus, among other things, and heard about IB for the first time at a meeting in which Jefferson teachers were discussing other programs they might try.

Crocker's time as a Jefferson vice principal had some entertaining moments. She was in charge of discipline, but the worst act of mayhem Jefferson students could think of was computer hacking, and they usually confessed the minute they were caught. She assigned them several hours of community service, often tutoring at a nearby elementary school, and they went off happy, knowing they could brag when they got to college about how bad they had been in high school.

It did not take Crocker long, once she got to Mount Vernon, to conclude that IB was even more rigorous than AP, and a great thing for the school. She realized that she would have to be attentive to a wide range of family backgrounds at Mount Vernon, where nearly 40 percent of the students were low income compared to just one percent at Jefferson. She had to worry if some students had had anything to eat before a test or had had a place to sleep the night before. If the school closed because of snow, she knew that some of her students, who depended on their federally funded free breakfast and lunch at Mount Vernon, would not eat that day.

As for the IB program, she was ready for those parents who wondered if the foreign-born courses were really as good as the better-known AP. She reminded them that she had been a math teacher, and had taught AP Calculus at Jefferson. "The IB covers more topics in depth, and is more rigorous in my opinion," she told them. "When I taught AP Calculus, for example, the first part of the test was multiple choice and the second part was six free-response questions. When you are doing a multiple choice question, you can know just enough to know that you can make the right choice by the process of elimination. But you have to really know the material, you can't just have an inkling, if you are going to answer a question on the IB exam, because they don't have multiple choice."

"I could say on an AP exam, find the derivative of y equals $2x$ squared and I could pick one of the five answers, but the IB approach would be, tell me why would you want to take the derivative of y equals $2x$ squared. What would you do with the derivative? The AP still does some of that, but not to the same extent."

She told parents and students that she realized some colleges did not give as much credit for one-year IB courses as they did for one-year AP courses, but that was a temporary problem that would go away as soon as the colleges realized their discriminatory policy made no sense. The colleges still gave credit for two-year IB courses, and had great respect for students who received the IB diploma. And once college professors realized how robust were the critical-thinking skills of IB students, they often allowed them to move to more challenging courses right away.

The Theory of Knowing
Paganini

In room A103, just down the hall from Rushing's history class, Will Crawford welcomed students to his after-school section of Theory of Knowledge. There were many difficulties in making an IB schedule work. Some students found no time during the regular day for TOK, so Crawford, just thirty years old and in his fourth year at Mount Vernon, volunteered to teach them after school, meaning that in 2004 he had six classes rather than the usual five.

There were nine students in the class. On this day all but one were present, seven girls and one boy. The class included one Asian American, one African American and one Hispanic American.

The day's TOK lesson dealt with music, an obsession for Crawford. He had played trumpet in college, had even jammed with Wynton Marsalis, and was eager to help his students prepare the art presentation. He told them to watch carefully as he modeled a presentation that afternoon so they would know how to organize their own presentations. Their work would be the first step to create the presentation required of all TOK students.

"I am going to play a piece of music," he said. "Most of you don't know what this song is, and we are going to then play the song again and see how your understanding of the song has changed." He wrote on the white board: "Artist vs. Audience." He told them there had to be a balance between satisfying yourself as an artist and pleasing the people who would hear or see your art.

The piece of music, he said, was "Moto Perpetuo" by Paganini. He pushed a few keys on the computer on his desk and the breathy sounds of a trumpet filled the classroom with an almost impossibly rapid succession of sixteenth notes. The music bounced off the cinderblock walls, too fast to imagine a human playing the instrument.

Crawford wrote on the board:

Ways of Knowing

Emotion _____
Perception _____
Language _____
Reason _____

"Now," he said, "give me your general impressions."

A girl said, "It didn't sound like he even took a breath."

This pleased Crawford. "He didn't! It's amazing that you noticed that."

He asked the class, "What does the title mean?"

"Perpetual motion," a girl said.

"Right. It just keeps going and going and going."

He pointed to the four ways of knowing on the board and asked, "What is the emotion of this song?"

The boy in the class said, "It's cheerful."

Crawford said, "Someone in the sixth period class said it made her nervous."

A girl said, "It sounds like an insect."

They discussed the perception dimension on the list. The passage seemed very fast, Crawford said, but if they were musicians, their perception might be different.

He came to language. "I just have here the illegally copied, I mean, legally photocopied sheet music." It was indeed all sixteenth notes, and hard to imagine how anyone could play it accurately.

When he came to the last item on the list, reason, he tried to be helpful. "Is there any logic or reason to the music?" he asked.

"If you can read music, what it is is a series of arpeggiated chords. It is very busy, up and down, but it makes sense."

He told them that it was Marsalis, his idol, who was playing on the recording. "There is a technique called circular breathing," he said. Marsalis was playing as he breathed, a remarkable feat.

Paganini, he explained, was a violinist, one of the best of his era. He sometimes composed music so difficult that few musicians other than himself could play it, and "Moto Perpetuo" was a good example. So this piece, clearly, emphasized the artist more than the audience. It was hard to interpret the melody. It was almost a stunt, a way to show off one's technique. "It's not necessarily something you are going to hum," Crawford said.

He pointed to the presentation rubric he had handed out. It was in four parts, five points maximum for each part. First were knowledge issues: what problems of knowledge are reflected in the artwork selected? Second was quality of analysis: what is the point of view, what is the bias, what justifies the main points? Third was knowledge at work: applying the principles learned in the course to the issues raised by the artwork. Fourth was a clarification of the argument, with a conclusion that wraps it all up. The sheet of paper reminded the students that they needed Crawford's approval "for any art that could be considered controversial."

He said they might not be able to hit all four ways of knowing in their presentation, but should try as many as they could. In the Paganini piece, for instance, the issue of language—a term nonmusicians rarely applied to music—could inspire an interesting discussion. "My dad, he was not a musician. He couldn't carry a pitch in a bucket," Crawford said. "But when he looked at a sheet of music he said there should be a better system. I think, however, that is a very useful system."

There was more discussion—of the different ways of interpreting a piece of art, of the different intentions of composers, of the many forms of knowledge. The bell rang and Crawford sent them off, long after their classmates had finished for the day, warning them that time was pressing. "I want to have by the end of the next class an idea of what you want to do," he said.

Still Pushing at Mount Vernon

On August 25, the first day of school for teachers in 2003, Dan Coast called a meeting of the IB faculty at Mount Vernon High to talk about the new year.

The school's reputation had been significantly enhanced by the IB program. Just two months before it had made *Newsweek*'s list of the most challenging high schools in America. It was number 309, putting it in the top 2 percent of the 25,000 U.S. public high schools, as measured by participation in college-level tests. Most of the schools below it on the list had much wealthier student bodies, such as Burlingame High on the San Francisco Peninsula, Grosse Pointe North in the Detroit suburbs, Oak Park and River Forest outside Chicago, and Central Bucks East High near Philadelphia.

But Coast did not want to rest on past achievements. He told the faculty the same thing they had heard from Calhoon, and what most of them believed: IB at Mount Vernon did not have enough students from the minority and low-income ranks of the student body.

"I want to see enrollment increase, particularly minority enrollment," he said. He noted that the county school headquarters had created something called Target 3, a general call for more minority participation in all kinds of challenging programs. At Mount Vernon that meant IB. "I truly believe that most if not every single student in this building can take at least one IB course, and probably more," he said.

At Back to School night, Coast had an African American student, one of his full-diploma stars, give a presentation on why IB was good for nearly everyone. There were panel discussions and meetings with minority parents and with the counselors who were advising students on what classes to take.

At every meeting with students he had the same message: "You can succeed in IB. If you are thinking about college, you need to find your favorite, strongest class and look at how the IB track can get you there, because it is not too late. It is not too late for any student. There is no gate-keeping here. There is no door that will slam shut on you."

He realized that not everyone on the Mount Vernon staff was comfortable with letting students risk failure in a very demanding program. He had heard the story of the counselor who had not encouraged Breigh Miller, who had just earned a full diploma, to enroll in pre-IB when she first arrived. He did not think any of his IB teachers had any hidden doubts, but he could never be sure.

He wanted to get every student into the program who needed to be there, but he knew from his own slow growth as a teacher that the most worthwhile and important things, if done right, took time. He had high expectations for himself and the program, but he did not think those expectations would be met until four or five years down the road. He thought that when people saw the way he operated and sensed his commitment, more of them would accept his ideas. Having seen what Calhoon's quiet persistence had done for IB, Coast was convinced that the coordinator's personality was an essential element of success. He hoped he wouldn't fall short.

To increase enrollment, he had to use every tool at his disposal and rally the four key groups—students, teachers, counselors, and parents. Some students would slip through the cracks if he did not have all four constituencies in sync. He himself had to be very visible and accessible, going to all the meetings and being particularly active at the middle school, Walt Whitman, from where most of the new pre-IB ninth graders would come.

Coast realized that some students would fail when given this opportunity, but he believed just being in the IB program, and giving it a try, would plant a seed that would bear fruit. He had recently gotten a call from a student, a very bright kid, who had graduated in 2000. He was, without any doubt, the worst IB student Coast had ever had. He had never gotten better than a D in IB Biology, and his score on the IB test had been a 2. He was a nice young man, but he skipped many classes and did not study.

But when the student called, it was to thank Coast for all that the teacher had done for him. The young graduate had not gone to college immediately. His grades made that a difficult transition, but he had worked and kept reading, influenced by some of the values he had seen exemplified at his old high school. And finally, he told Coast, he had been accepted to a college in the Midwest that was willing to let him into a premed program.

"Mick," Coast said, "you are the worst student I ever had. But I loved you, and I enjoyed your company. I knew you could do it. I am so happy you are moving in that direction."

With teachers, Coast had only to allude to his early struggles to make the point that while IB helps and challenges students, it also helps and challenges the professionals who teach them. "I grew so much professionally when I came to Fairfax County," he told them, "partly due to what the county demanded of me—the technology, the standards—but also because of what IB expected of me."

He found that examining the initial grades that new IB teachers handed out to students helped him prevent problems. He looked at the DF ratios, the percentage of first marking period grades that were either Ds or Fs. For one teacher, the portion was 31 percent, too high in Coast's opinion. He looked at the profiles of her students. They were juniors, new to IB, and some of them had not done well as sophomores, but the teacher had decided to hold them to the high IB standard right away, and Coast thought that ill-advised.

He went to talk to her and share some of his own tricks. He told her about handing back his Ds and Fs on his first few labs, but telling them he would give them a chance to rewrite them before logging them in on the computer. If they got an A or B the second time, he put it down on their record. If the work was still below that quality, he had them do it again. "You have to get them to understand the mastery level before making them accountable for it," he told the new IB teacher.

He expected her to be defensive, but she listened carefully and did not try to pick a fight with him. She said she would have to consider his approach. She was an excellent teacher. Her students' scores on the state SOL test in previous years had been the highest in her department. She held her students to that standard, and they met it. She would hold her students to the IB standard and the same thing would happen, but not in the first quarter.

He also had a few battles to fight with the colleges. One of his graduates could not get credit at Coast's alma mater, Virginia Tech, for a one-year, standard level IB math course he had taken. On the university's web site, it said the university gave credit for a standard level exam if it was part of a student's full diploma program. But if the student had taken it just for a certificate, there would be no credit, even though it was the same course.

That was an isolated case, Coast thought. Most of the colleges understood what they were doing.

And the results were so much better than they had ever been. In 2003 Mount Vernon High School had had 29 diploma candidates, and 24 had received the full diploma. In 2004, 191 juniors and 150 seniors were in the IB program, nearly half of all the students in those classes.

Coast was hiring more teachers, and looking for ways to use the test results, as Calhoon had done, to see how each teacher was doing. Not only were the IB test results a check on progress, but they were a great motivator.

The IB Biology exam was the most difficult test he had ever given to students in his professional career. If he had not had those dismal scores to look at during his first few years, he would have thought he was doing a great job. With no exam, there was no feedback. But once he knew what was happening, he could do something about it, and he expected that was what would happen with all of his new teachers too.

Too Many Tests for Rosenfeld

Emmet Rosenfeld found himself increasingly dissatisfied with teaching at Mount Vernon, and it wasn't the IB program's fault. His English classes opened up the world of literature for students who would otherwise have not read much at all. IB, he thought, cracked open the canon of old-style teaching and let good things spill out.

He liked the breadth of the assessments in IB. There were oral tests, timed written tests, and untimed essay tests and projects. It was a great way to evaluate students' work. You could see someone's mind if you looked at what they wrote. It was better than seeing how many right answers they had on a vocabulary test.

He also liked the variety of young people in the program. Having a self-selected pool of students was good, he thought. That meant they worked harder than if they were in a course, like regular biology or history, that had a state test they had to pass to graduate. After a while he stopped noticing how ethnically diverse his students were, but when he stopped to think about it, the beneficial effects were evident. He at first thought IB was just a political Band-Aid, an impressive-sounding program that might persuade a few middle-class families to stay, and leave the mistaken impression the school district cared about its less affluent neighborhoods. But IB surprised him by proving to be a meaningful way to teach and learn. Even the CAS, the community service requirement, was a plus. It was not student initiated, but it made sense to him, and Rosenfeld eventually became the CAS coordinator at Mount Vernon.

But he worried about the work load, even for IB students who had volunteered for it. He saw some kids buckle and start to do mediocre work in class, just to get it done, just to get some sleep. Many of them were also doing a school play and a sport and the band, and he thought it was too much. Calhoon had made it a top priority to try to talk IB students out of extra activities, but she could not order them to drop band, and some of them were very stubborn.

Rosenfeld thought in many cases the problem wasn't the students, but those teachers who seemed to be determined to make their class the toughest in the school. He thought some teachers, insecure about their skills, covered inadequacies with long homework assignments, some of them not very meaningful. Some teachers also seemed to take more pride than was proper in the growing prestige of the IB program, and liked the cutthroat parts of it more than they ought to have. They approved, for instance, of the winnowing process, which was pretty brutal. Usually about sixty or seventy Mount Vernon juniors would start the program, but only a couple of dozen would get the full diploma.

But Rosenfeld also remembered the many times former students came back to see him and the other IB teachers and said: College has been a breeze for me. I was very well prepared. The IB workload and time management requirements helped me.

So, Rosenfeld often said to himself, they do learn that, and that does work for a lot of kids.

He might have stayed at Mount Vernon longer if it had not been for the new Virginia Standards of Learning (SOL) tests. The IB tests were clever and deep and rewarded teachers who encouraged critical thinking. The SOL were, in his view, quite different—narrow multiple-choice tests not worth the time and effort.

He didn't mind his students having to take a state test. Of the 120 students he had in his last year at Mount Vernon, 2002-2003, only eight did not pass the SOL test in English for eleventh graders, and a couple of those did not even show up for it. He did not mind their scores going on their transcript. But he did mind the state making it such a high-stakes test, with students not able to graduate if they did not pass the English test and five others.

He thought some teachers found it too difficult to resist the temptation to focus their lessons on just the SOL tests. He thought they forced administrators to organize SOL training sessions that took teachers away from their classrooms. The tests had, for him, sucked much of the life out of school and poisoned his environment beyond what he would tolerate.

So he took his spinning plates and his fish food and his color codes and accepted a job at a local private school.

He would have a chance to teach eighth graders, a challenge that appealed to him because it meant he could inspire a love of reading and writing in students even before they got to high school. He would be able to start an outdoor program that linked school to the world. And no longer would he have to spend even a second of his time worrying about the SOLs.

The IB Credit Problem

The success of IB at Mount Vernon and Stuart high schools in Fairfax County led more than a dozen Washington area schools to adopt the program by 2001, but not all parents were sold on its virtues. Anne Hall, for instance, arranged for her daughter to leave Fairfax County's South Lakes High School, an IB school, twice a week to take an Advanced Placement course at another county high school.

And, with the support of a few other parents and teachers, Hall demanded that Fairfax school officials explain why they were replacing AP with IB at other schools without a vote of parents and without more research on the failure of many colleges to give credit for IB courses as frequently as they did for AP.

Hall said that although Fairfax school administrators told parents that IB and AP were the same, "several teachers have told me that AP math and science courses are more beneficial to students who wish to pursue math and sciences in college."

The differences, real and otherwise, between AP and IB were becoming important to parents and students throughout the country. The two college-level high school programs had taken hold, and yet even some AP and IB educators were not clear on how they compared. The college professors who decided which courses got how much college credit were often ignorant of what was learned in each program, and what was on the AP and IB tests they were assessing.

Without exception, college admissions officers said that in one important area, AP and IB were of very great and equal value. Students who had taken AP or IB courses were more likely to be admitted to selective colleges than students who had not taken the courses. IB looked just as good as AP on a transcript, admissions officials said, and if a student had taken the full six courses required for an IB diploma, so much the better.

Martin A. Wilder, vice president for enrollment at the University of Mary Washington in Fredericksburg and a leading national expert on admissions for the National Association for College Admission Counseling, said IB and AP "are both on a par in terms of the basic level of challenge."

But parents like Hall identified one problem in the IB program that also bothered IB officials and counselors in IB schools. Many colleges made it easier for AP students than for IB students to get college credit for their work.

Since IB was used in only about 400 schools in the United States, compared with about 14,000 for AP, many college officials were less familiar with it, and were not even sure who wrote the regulations for IB credit on their own university websites. When asked why they gave credit for an AP course but not for a similar grade in a similar IB course, college officials often said they had no explanation, or that the rules were drawn up by someone else long ago. Some college officials said they had granted credit to incoming IB students who protested the discrepancy, but saw no reason, at least for the time being, to change the rules that favored AP.

For most students applying to selective colleges, and their parents, getting into the school of their choice was more important than getting extra college credits once they were admitted. IB students had such success in admission that the apparent discrimination against IB in credit-giving did not affect the program's steady growth.

"IB parents are far less concerned with any future college credits," said Dick Reed, whose daughter Sara had been part of the IB program at Fairfax County's Edison High School. "IB teaches students to ask questions and to probe more and more deeply into a subject to get at its roots, and then to use that knowledge as the basis for interpretation, interpolation, and action."

One of the most telling indicators was the growth of both IB and AP at Richard Montgomery High School in Rockville, Maryland. The school had an IB magnet program that drew students from all over the county, but it also gave many AP exams. In 2003, Richard Montgomery gave 558 IB tests and 1,447 AP tests. Because of the greater likelihood of getting credit for an AP exam, many of the school's IB students took both the IB exam and the AP exam in the subject they were studying. Many said the IB exam was just as difficult as the AP test and sometimes harder.

Jack Thirolf, one of the Richard Montgomery IB students, took the AP and IB tests in economics in 2000 after taking the Standard Level IB Economics course. Thirolf got the highest grade possible, a 5, on the AP test and the next-to-highest grade, a 6, on the IB test. He said he thought the IB test was more difficult. He said the AP test asked mostly about theories, while the IB test also demanded knowledge and analysis of situations in developing countries and other issues.

Yet at Mary Washington, a student like Thirolf would get credit for only the AP test and no credit for the IB test no matter how high the score. Like many other colleges, Mary Washington did not recognize any Standard Level IB courses, which, like AP courses, usually cover just one year's work. The college insisted that IB students take two-year Higher Level courses, and score at least a 5 on the 7-point IB exam to receive credit. The same students could receive credit with only a 3 on an AP exam after a one-year course, even though many experts considered a 3 on AP the equivalent of a 4 on IB.

Wilder, the vice president for enrollment at Mary Washington, said he could not explain the discrepancy at his college. At Cornell University, Steve Chase, associate chairman of the mathematics department, was similarly uncertain why the school gave no credit for any Standard Level IB math tests, even those with the highest scores, and required much higher scores on Higher Level IB exams for credit than for AP exams. Asked if the policy had not been carefully examined, he said, "That may be the case."

Hall said she thought IB science and math courses did not prepare students adequately for college, which was why her daughter, a senior, was taking an AP Chemistry course at another school rather than the IB Chemistry course at South Lakes. But officials at Cornell University, Duke University, and Mary Washington said they were unaware of any such problem with IB Chemistry, and a University of Florida study of its upper-level chemistry course indicated IB success. Only freshmen with at least a 3 on the AP Chemistry exam or a 4 in the IB Chemistry exam were admitted to the course. The study said 91.7 percent of the IB students had a B or better in the first part of the sequence and 70 percent had a B or better in the second part, compared to 58.3 percent and 42.2 percent respectively for all students in those courses.

Glaze, having become head of advanced academic programs for Fairfax County, continued to argue that IB was at least as strong as AP. She said that Fairfax decided to let individual principals, after consulting with parents and teachers, decide whether to offer AP or IB but that the county could not afford to run the programs simultaneously in individual schools, except for Robinson Secondary School, which was so large it could accommodate both.

The controversy over credit did not seem to hurt relations between IB and AP. Harpo Hanson, the AP official who helped start IB, died in 1996 but his cooperative attitude lived on in the many educators, both on the IB and the AP side, who had worked with him. Both the College Board, owners of the AP, and IB North America had their offices in Manhattan, and the two sides often talked and even had joint conferences.

In 2002 IB North America and the College Board went so far as to produce together a brochure to help students, parents, and teachers trying to sort out the differences between them and make the proper individual choice. It said that both programs were rigorous and devoted to educational excellence. It said both were highly regarded by U.S. universities. In schools that had both programs, the brochure noted, combinations of courses were possible, such as two IB certificate courses along with a couple of APs.

IB officials said they were not obsessing over the slow progress toward equal credit policies for both AP and IB, since the IB students usually managed to get the courses they wanted anyway. And in the end, they said, the competition helped both organizations, and the students they served. They all remembered being told by Hanson that when his children reached high school age, he gave them the facts and let them decide which program they wanted.

Two chose IB. Two chose AP. And in each case, Hanson said, it was just the right choice.

Teaching "Socialism, Disarmament, Radical Environmentalism, and Moral Relativism"

The failure of universities to give credit for one-year IB courses was not the only thing that bothered critics of the program. Over the years, some parents, educators, and policy makers had expressed concern about the sexual and moral content of some suggested readings in IB English—Isabel Allende's *The House of the Spirits* came under fire—as well as what seemed to them an IB commitment to world peace, and close ties to the United Nations. They said they sensed a leftist, ultra-liberal bias that might lead IB students to accept without question the rightness of a future world ruled by one government.

George Archibald, an education reporter for the *Washington Times*, explored this perspective from parents and other IB critics in three articles that appeared January 18, 2004. One of Archibald's articles described the international focus of IB and its fondness for student participation in learning, and said it seemed to be at odds with the views of some educators associated with the Bush administration, despite the fact that IB programs had recently received a federal grant from the U.S. Education Department. A second article said parents in Reston, Virginia, were complaining about what they said was IB teaching of socialism and moral relativism at a local middle school and high school. The third article told the story of Woodson High School's rejection of IB (see chapter 27).

The lead paragraph of Archibald's main article said: "The Bush administration has begun issuing grants to help spread a United Nations–sponsored school program that aims to become a 'universal curriculum' for teaching global citizenship, peace studies and equality of world cultures."

It said the U.S. Education Department had awarded a $1.2 million grant to implement the IB Middle Years Program in Arizona, Massachusetts, and New York. It quoted Education Secretary Rod Paige praising the program, but Archibald said that "some educators are skeptical."

The article quoted former Reagan administration education official Chester E. Finn Jr. as saying he was "a wee bit put off" by IB's "one-worldism and fashionable leftism of their social studies courses, but they weren't worse than what regular American curricula were peddling and the academic expectations were far more rigorous."

Archibald quoted U.S. Education Department spokeswoman Susan M. Aspey as saying the funding approval for the $1.2 million grant for IB was recommended by "independent peer reviewers," and was ranked third out of 117 applications by outside academic experts "chosen specifically for their deep knowledge of the types of programs under review." Syl McNinch Jr., a retired budget officer for the National Science Foundation, told Archibald that many federal education peer-reviewers of grant applications were "hard left-leaners."

Archibald described a 1996 agreement between IBO and the United Nations Educational, Scientific and Cultural Organization to create a "universal framework for peace education." The UNESCO announcement at the time said the project participants "see education as the principal vehicle for developing and inculcating the habits of peace in school-age children."

Ian Hill, coauthor of this book, was quoted in the article as saying that the role of international education and culture was to fulfill the vision of UNESCO's constitution in its opening words: "Since wars begin in the minds of men, it is in the minds of men that the defenses of peace must be constructed." Hill added, "We cannot hide from one another and we can't eliminate dissident groups. We have to learn to live together."

Bradley W. Richardson, director of IB North America, told Archibald the program's "ties to the United Nations and

UNESCO are both historic and collegial." He said, "We have an advisory status as [a nongovernmental organization] with UNESCO, but that relationship does not extend to curriculum development or assessments. . . . IB's association with UNESCO should not signal anything sinister or anti-American."

The article said Richardson denied that IB's courses had a political or social-activist agenda. "While the course requires that these 'politically correct' questions be engaged, it in no way (nor does the assessment) requires any particular response to the questions. A 'conservative' answer well done will always score higher than a 'liberal' answer poorly done," he said.

In the article on Reston parents, Archibald quoted part of a letter to the Reston Connection, a local newspaper, written in 2003 by Jeanne Geiger, one of the people concerned about the IB programs at Langston Hughes Middle School and South Lakes High School. "Administrators do not tell you that the current IB program for ages three through grade 12 promotes socialism, disarmament, radical environmentalism, and moral relativism, while attempting to undermine Christian religious values and national sovereignty," the letter said.

The article quoted Rena J. Berlin, IB coordinator at Langston Hughes, as saying, "All students who learn how to think globally, how to make connections between subjects, and how to 'learn how to learn' will be better prepared to be IB diploma students when they get to the 11th grade. . . . After all, it is our students who will change the world and we need to allow them to be the fine citizens of America and the world that they have the potential to be."

The third article told the story of Woodson High's rejection of IB and included this quote from E. J. "Nell" Hurley, a leader of the successful effort to stop the removal of AP courses from that school: "The admissions director of the University of Virginia told us, 'If you are at an IB school and you are not going for the IB diploma, don't waste your time applying to U-Va. or any other top-rated schools. Your child's application will go to the bottom of the admissions pile.'"

Archibald did not quote any U-Va. officials reacting to the statement, but when asked about it after the *Washington Times* articles were published, U-Va. dean of admission John A. Blackburn said Hurley's quote was "incorrect and misleading."

"I did not make the remark and would quickly point out that we admit many IB students without the IB diploma as long as they have taken a full selection of the IB courses offered, known as IB certificates, and have done well in them," Blackburn said. "Just as with AP courses, we encourage students to take a solid selection of them, particularly in English, math, science, history and foreign language. We consider the IB diploma to be excellent preparation for the work here at U-Va., but for those students who do not take on that challenge, we expect them to take a rigorous program from within the offerings of the school's IB curriculum."

Asked about Blackburn's denial, Hurley provided a copy of the minutes from the Oct. 10, 1999, meeting with college representatives at Hayfield Secondary School that led her to say what she said to Archibald. The minutes show that the U-Va. official that night was not Blackburn, but Stephen Farmer, then an admissions officer at the university. The minutes said,

> The UVA rep noted that, in his view, there is no more rigorous course of advanced studies in the high school level than the IB diploma. . . . At UVA, they are looking to see that a student is taking the most demanding course of study available at that school. At an IB school, being an IB diploma candidate is a way to demonstrate this. At an AP school, taking several AP courses is a way to do this. In response to a parent question, the rep indicated that this would typically mean 4-5 AP courses. . . . A student at an IB school who is taking only a few IB courses and a student at an AP school who is taking only a few AP courses would be at a comparative disadvantage unless there were extenuating circumstances. While the IB Diploma is impressive to UVA, they do admit students who have not taken the full diploma load.

Shown a copy of the minutes, Blackburn said Farmer had stated U-Va. policy well, and Hurley had misreported his words. Farmer, when contacted four years after the event, agreed that

Hurley had gotten it wrong in her *Washington Times* quote. Hurley said she had not done so, but had been handicapped by trying to paraphrase for Archibald something she had heard four years before.

Asked for his thoughts on that article almost a year after it was published, Archibald said:

> My reporting for the *Washington Times* showed incontrovertibly that parents and students who objected to the International Baccalaureate curriculum were correct: College admissions officers across the U.S. did not consider IB courses on a par with Advanced Placement, so high school students in the IB program suffered in college applications. Also, the overwhelming number of U.S. colleges did not give course credit for standard IB courses, as they did for all AP courses, so high school students who spent years to get the full IB certificate were badly short-changed in losing credits and monetary benefit for upwards of a year's worth of college course and tuition credit, while AP students were not.

Shortly after the Archibald articles appeared, Thomas Sowell of Stanford University's Hoover Institution wrote a syndicated column saying, "Parents in Fairfax, Virginia, have succeeded in getting rid of one of the endless series of fad programs that distract American public schools from real education in real subjects. Like most fad programs, this one had a high-sounding name: The International Baccalaureate Curriculum."

He repeated Geiger's description of IB from the *Washington Times* article, and congratulated "the parents in Fairfax" who "had the backbone to get this junk program thrown out of their school," an apparent reference to Woodson High, although he noted that "the battle is still raging in nearby Reston, Virginia, where the education bureaucrats are determined to create a generation of internationalists."

Paul Regnier, spokesman for the Fairfax County Schools, and Bernie Glaze, as specialist for advanced academic programs in the county, began to get calls from around the country asking if it was true that Fairfax County had dropped IB. Regnier asked Sowell for a correction. "Eight of our 24 high schools currently

offer the IB program, with excellent results and strong community support," he told Sowell in an email. "The IB is far from a
'fad' and has been successful in many American schools for many
years. One American high school that has had the program for
over 25 years is George Mason High School in the City of Falls
Church, a small school system that is our neighbor. You will find,
if you check, that their graduates go on to many of the top universities in the nation, where they are very successful—and 25
years does not sound like a fad to me."

45

Rousseau in Locust Valley

One day in March 2004, Lisa McLoughlin, a real estate broker and parent living on Long Island's North Shore, received a glossy eight-by-ten-inch brochure in the mail. It said that her daughter's school, Locust Valley High School, had adopted something called the International Baccalaureate program.

She did not know what that was, but she was a very active parent with a deep suspicion of educational fads and not much confidence in her local school's administration. She started to check it out, and her first impressions were not good. The advent of IB, she learned, would mean a significant drop in the number of AP courses at the 650-student public school. Locust Valley High was also eliminating all honors courses for eleventh and twelfth graders, since they could take IB instead.

Before long, she had written a piece for the local newspaper saying the school had "thrown the baby out with the bathwater and embraced the tacit socialist movement to dumb down America under the guise of improvement."

McLoughlin was one of a small but possibly growing number of Americans with longstanding concerns about American culture and education who had come to see IB as an enemy. They focused with apprehension on the word "international" in IB's name, while a much larger group of IB supporters emphasized the word "baccalaureate" as a sign of rigor and future college success.

It was a battle between people who thought the country was too soft and people who thought the country was too dumb. Clashes between the two groups were rare. People who shared

McLoughlin's concerns rarely came in contact with IB because it was in so few schools. And they found many instances of left-leaning instruction in American schools without IB programs, since teachers, polls showed, tended to be more politically liberal than Americans in general. But there was a good chance the disputes over the ideology of IB would become more frequent as the program in America, encompassing almost half of all the IB schools in the world, got bigger.

George Archibald's IB series in the *Washington Times* was one sign of the distrust of the program in some minds, but it was not the first time IB officials had encountered such feelings. In 1987 the future IB North America regional director, Bradley Richardson, was in a Minnesota suburb, working as an IB representative to help a public high school create an IB program. He was meeting with the members of the mathematics department and asked one teacher, who had been very quiet and seemingly troubled, if there was something he wanted to say.

The man began to swear at him. "I think this is a Communist plot to take over the country," Richardson recalled the man saying, "and I don't want anything to do with you. My plan is to teach an average curriculum to average students so they can become average citizens." Then the man walked out of the room. The other teachers shook their heads in surprise. "He hardly ever says anything," one of them told Richardson.

There have been more complaints since. In 2002 Charlene Sanders of Hot Springs, Arkansas, said that educators in her area were wrong to adopt an IB program that was, she said, closely tied to a pantheistic religion called Theosophy. She said local educators had "invited the fox into the henhouse."

Gregg Thompson, principal of North Little Rock High School West, told Sanders that he had grown up in the country and remembered that when the fox is in the henhouse, the chickens squawk, the dogs bark, and the owner immediately "makes getting the fox 'Job 1.'" Thompson said that despite IB's arrival, "our chickens aren't squawking, the dogs aren't barking, no feathers are flying, and our owners say 'Job 1' is preparing our chickens to produce more eggs than the chickens across the big pond."

"Is there a fox?" he said. "Only time will tell."

In 2004, anti-IB activists in the Owego Apalachin, New York, school district successfully prevented the start of a Middle Year Program and a Primary Years Program. Both programs had been popular in Cherry Hill, New Jersey, where the Owego Apalachin superintendent, Mychael Willon, had last served, but when letters to the editor of the *Binghamton Press & Sun-Bulletin* began to appear, suggesting IB was anti-American, the negative reaction led to the rejection of the district's budget by voters, and a task force organized by Willon to reexamine the issue seemed unlikely to reinstate the two programs.

About the same time, McLoughlin was confronting Locust Valley's plan to install IB. She did not consider herself an expert on educational matters. She did not, she said, have a Ph.D., an Ed.D., or even an M.A. or a B.A., but was a "middle-aged, middle-class mother of a 21-year-old son and a 15-year-old daughter" and "a registered Republican with Libertarian leanings who is fond of family, capitalism, property ownership and proud to be an American."

In the Locust Valley school system she had volunteered as chair for a community task force on substance abuse prevention, served as a PTA vice president, founded an elementary science fair, and even run, albeit unsuccessfully, for the school board. She knew how to reach people, and her opinion piece in the Locust Valley Leader, written under a pseudonym to avoid unwelcome attention to her daughter, hit the district hard. She said she thought the IB program was too expensive and had not earned the adjective "prestigious" that so many local school administrators were attaching to it. Changing the Locust Valley course structure particularly concerned her, she said. "The elimination of the honors track presents underclassmen with a dilemma when planning for their final two years in high school," she wrote. "Should former honors students opt for the rigorous and intensive IB 'programme' leaving little time for other activities? Or, should they drop to the regents level where they can sail through by making A's and having time for sports and other interests?"

She found George Archibald's IB articles on the Internet and launched her own investigation of the Swiss-based organization. One document that caught her eye was IBO director general George Walker's keynote address to the IB North America regional conference in Victoria, British Columbia, on July 20, 2002. His title was "Geneva's Contribution to World Peace: Ideals, Individuals and Institutions." In the speech, the one-time chemistry teacher and school administrator—an Englishman like his predecessor Alec Peterson—expressed admiration for eighteenth-century French philosopher Jean-Jacques Rousseau, which McLoughlin found disquieting.

"Hmmm," she said later in an email about her research.

> I wonder which parts of Rousseau's Social Contract Walker finds most appealing and worth endorsing. Would it be Rousseau's assertion that "Sovereignty is the power of the General Will expressed for the common good of the whole community" or that sovereignty is "inalienable, indivisible and *unrepresentative*"? Maybe it was Rousseau's belief that Christianity should be held suspect and considered a divisive and separatist force in European society, perpetually threatening to destroy the nation-state system. Or perhaps that ownership of private property is a good thing, as long as "his own estate is always subordinate to the right of community over all." Now granted, I'm not a philosopher or an historian, but somehow the words "collectivism" and "communism" seem to spring to mind.

The Locust Valley High School principal, Richard Shear, defended the IB program in the newspaper and before the school board when McLoughlin rose at a meeting to complain. He said the district had been looking at IB for several years.

> The key question I asked the educators involved in the decision was, if your child was going to school in Locust Valley would you want IB or AP? There were approximately six educators who had returned from an IB training session and the decision was unani-

mous to pursue IB. We held a faculty meeting and presented our
findings and the faculty endorsed the program. A number of people
endorsed it reluctantly, but they did endorse it. We went to the parent council and the high school site based management team—with
parents and students—and they endorsed the program.

He said the school did not have the money or manpower to
run two large and separate AP and IB programs, although it
would keep some AP courses in topics not covered by IB. As for
the honors courses, he said they "truly didn't challenge students
and since we have open enrollment in IB and AP, . . . honors
classes should not be part of the program in the junior and senior
year. The parents on the site based team were very strong in their
belief that if honors remained in the program, numerous students would drop IB as soon as it asked students to put in a maximum effort."

Locust Valley was a prosperous community with very few
minority families and fewer than 10 percent of students poor
enough to qualify for federal lunch subsidies. It had a much
higher percentage of affluent, college-educated parents than
Mount Vernon High school, where in 2004 43 percent of the
students qualified for lunch subsidies and 47 percent were black
or Hispanic. And yet Mount Vernon was ranked slightly higher
than Locust Valley on the 2003 *Newsweek* list of America's most
challenging high schools, based on AP and IB participation.
Mount Vernon's IB program, despite its large number of disadvantaged students, was number 309 in the country while Locust
Valley's AP program was number 330, both in the top 2 percent
of all American high schools.

Still, McLoughlin thought that IB was too expensive and too
ideological for her community. She handed out fliers at the
school when classes started in September announcing an upcom-
ing meeting, and got into an argument with administrators about
her right to do so. She said the Woodson High story had inspired
her, and she planned to keep fighting to reinstate honors and AP.

At the headquarters of IB North America in New York,
regional director Richardson decided it was time to compose a

comprehensive summary of what IB was about. This, he said, would help parents, teachers, and students confused by what they were hearing. Officials at the U.S. Education Department had requested just such a handout to send to callers complaining about the $1.2 million federal grant to the Middle Years Program mentioned in the Archibald article. The result of the IB effort was a twenty-page document, in English and French, called "Overview of International Baccalaureate in the United States."

It said the organization was committed to "international understanding, intellectual rigor and high academic achievement." To counter charges of anti-Americanism, it said, "The IBO believes that relevant education begins with an understanding and appreciation of one's own culture. From that perspective, comes an understanding and appreciation of differing cultures and histories. This belief is emphasized in the structure and curriculum of the IB programmes."

It quoted endorsements of IB from, among others, U.S. Education Secretary Rod Paige, Harvard University Director of Undergraduate Admission Marlyn McGrath Lewis, and Fairfax County advanced academic programs coordinator Bernie Glaze.

It also noted, for those who suggested IB did not have America's interests at heart, that the organization often worked with the Military Child Education Coalition (MCEC). It quoted Mary Keller, Executive Director of MCEC, as saying, "From the very beginning, MCEC has encouraged military children to pursue a rigorous academic programme. One programme we have singled out for attention is IB. We encourage military students to look for demanding courses that challenge them academically as well as programmes 'without borders' that are available worldwide—the IB programme fits both requirements!"

But McLoughlin was not impressed. "Do they really believe that one's own cultural understanding is something the children received from their parents and that it is something IBO seeks to change in the Primary Years? It would seem so," she said. "They also state that there is no encroachment on the school's management, governance or instruction. This is clearly not so, as the school must comply with assessment procedures and follow course guidelines as presumably outlined *somewhere* which directly encroaches on instruction."

Shear said that McLoughlin's doubts were not shared by the high school, where 25 percent of the juniors signed up for the full IB diploma program. "As far as we know," he said, "we are the only public school to start the program in such an ambitious manner. . . . Regardless of how many finish the diploma, we believe that students who challenge the courses with appropriate support will be enriched. . . . We walked our talk and encouraged students regardless of prior tracking to pursue their dreams."

McLoughlin suggested, however, that IB and its participating schools will have to provide more information than what she considered the vague overview, and be ready to answer all questions in a more forthright manner. "As a parent," McLoughlin said,

> I am able to sit down with my child and go through a high school course catalog of what course offerings there are for her next year and help her with her selection. I can read a description of the topics covered. This has not been the case with IB so far.
>
> For anyone in the position of deciding whether or not this program is an appropriate fit for their community, I don't think it can be done honestly without knowing what they are accepting by embracing IB.

46

The Rise of IB

By 2004, after more than three decades of growth throughout the world and particularly rapid development in the United States, International Baccalaureate programs had reached 116 countries. There were 426 high schools in the United States and 89 in Canada, slightly less than half of the world total of about 1,100 authorized to offer the IB diploma. In the United States 49 schools had the Middle Years Program and 30 the Primary Years Program.

The American total was less than 2 percent of the total number of high schools in the country, but IB's influence on American education had grown out of proportion to its numbers, at least as measured by media attention and prominence in the growing movement to quantify public school achievement.

In the 2003 *Newsweek* magazine list of America's Best High Schools there was a total of 113 IB schools. This was 14 percent of the extended list of 824 public schools with the strongest college-level test participation rates.

Throughout the world in 2004 there were 187,033 IB exams taken by 56,284 candidates. The number one school in total number of exams given was MARA College in Banting, Malaysia, with 2,100 tests. The leading American school, and number three in the world, was Robinson Secondary School in Fairfax County, with 1,281 IB exams. Mount Vernon ranked ninety-sixth in the world on that list, fifty-second among IB schools in the United States, and seventh among IB schools in Fairfax County.

In 2004, 81,182 IB exams were taken by 31,413 candidates in the United States. There were 7,790 IB diplomas awarded in the United States, a 76 percent success rate among diploma candidates. Nearly 81 percent of IB exams taken in American schools received grades of 4 or above.

The statistics impressed many educators, but American students, parents, and school administrators were more interested in how much IB schools were adding to students' chances for success in college and in life. A few small studies indicated preliminary, positive results. William Kolb, director of admissions for the University of Florida, analyzed the SAT scores of his freshmen in 1996 and found students from IB schools had an average SAT score of 1213, while those from AP programs averaged 1177 and those from standard college prep programs averaged 1158.

Kolb found that IB students were better prepared for the shock of college academic demands and suffered less of a drop in grade point average in their first year of college compared to what they had done in high school. The IB students on average had a GPA decline of from 3.8 to 3.3, only a 0.5 drop, while AP students dropped 0.8, from 3.9 to 3.1, and regular college prep students lost a whole grade point, from 3.6 to 2.6.

In the upper level chemistry course sequence at Florida, the percentage of freshmen who received Bs or better in the course after being admitted because of their IB credit was nearly twice as much as the percentage of Bs among all students in the course. Kolb found similarly superior performance for IB students in the university's expository writing, technical writing, pre-calculus, and analytic geometry and calculus courses. Studies at Marquette University in 1996 and 1997 and the College of William and Mary from 1990 to 1997 found higher college grade point averages for IB students when compared to the general student body.

Several studies in the 1990s and the 2000s indicated that introduction of IB to high schools energized Advanced Placement courses also, if the school was willing to maintain both AP and IB programs. At Vista High School in Vista, California, according to data collected between 1982 and 1995, the introduction of IB was followed by a sharp increase in student enrollment in honors, AP and IB courses. The same thing happened at South Side High School in Rockville Centre, New York, and Westwood High School in Austin, Texas.

Westwood also showed a significant jump in the percentage of students passing the Texas state test required for graduation after IB was introduced. Palmer High School in Colorado Springs, Colorado, reported an increase in average SAT and ACT scores after IB courses were established.

Linda M. Duevel, in her 1999 doctoral dissertation at Purdue University, said 87 percent of IB diploma graduates at twelve selective universities earned bachelor's degrees in five years or less, significantly above the average completion rate for those colleges. IB students reported very high levels of satisfaction from what they had learned in the program, she said, particularly in their ability to understand complex assignments (91 percent), ability to work independently (88 percent), and ability to organize their time (91 percent).

A survey by IB North America of selective universities found the acceptance rate of IB diploma candidates much higher than the acceptance rate for all applicants.

The best statistical profile of IB students came from an IB survey of 1,041 IB seniors in May 2001. They were attending twenty-eight high schools in Maryland, Virginia, South Carolina, and the District of Columbia. Fifty-six percent were diploma candidates and 44 percent were studying for certificates for some IB courses. The diploma candidates' passing rate on IB exams was 84 percent, higher than the 75 percent average for the United States. The certificate candidates had taken an average 2.31 exams each and had an average score of 4.24, while the diploma candidates in the survey averaged a score of 4.96 on each exam.

Sixty percent of the sampled students were female and 40 percent male, with no significant difference in their performance on the exams. Their ethnic breakdown was 65 percent non-Hispanic white, 14 percent African American, 12 percent Asian or Pacific Islander, 5 percent Hispanic, 1 percent Native American and 4

FALL 2002 UNIVERSITY ACCEPTANCE RATES

	Acceptance Rates	
University	*All Applicants*	*IB Applicants*
Harvard University	11%	14.4%
United States Naval Academy	11.67%	42.9%
Columbia University	12%	18.3%
Stanford University	12.6%	16.9%
Yale University	13%	19.5%
Brown University	17%	20.8%
Dartmouth College	20.7%	35.1%
California Institute of Technology	21%	40.7%
Washington University St. Louis	23.5%	68.5%
University of California at Berkeley	24%	47.6%
Northwestern University	32.9%	57.7%
University of Notre Dame	34.2%	41.4%
College of William and Mary	37%	55%
University of Virginia	38.1%	63.3%
Emory University	42%	82.1%
University of Maryland	43.5%	87%
University of Michigan at Ann Arbor	49%	73.4%
Reed College	55%	90.9%
Brigham Young University	60%	86.2%
Baylor University	81%	100%

percent other. Asked their socioeconomic status, 7 percent said high, 80 percent said middle, and 13 percent said low.

Educators at Mount Vernon High School, seeing that profile, noted that their high school had a much higher percentage of minority test takers, and were doing almost as well as that sample of mostly middle-class white students.

47

"You Can't Make Me Earn the Diploma"

In the winter of 2004 Mount Vernon held a Curriculum Fair, a night for students and parents to learn about the courses available to them in the next school year and sign up for those they wanted. Crocker, the principal, had a little speech for such occasions:

> When you sign up your child to be in the IB diploma program, you are not signing up to see how many credits they are going to get in their freshman year of college. You are signing up to see how well can we develop critical thinking skills, how well can we educate your child in all facets of education. If you are signing up to earn college credits, you have chosen IB for the wrong reason.

Some of the parents were confused by this, but as they learned more about IB, they began to understand what she was talking about. The idea was to build academic skills and interests so that Mount Vernon students would not only get to college, but graduate. Only half of American students who started college ever finished, and many of the dropouts lost heart when they could not handle the rigors of freshman year.

Crocker worked with Calhoon, and later Dan Coast, on more ways to lure uncertain students into IB so they could expand the number of students they were preparing for more choices in life. They knew one thing that scared students away from a difficult program was other students. Seniors loved to terrify freshmen with tales of endless homework assignments and impossible tests. So Crocker and her IB coordinators found successful members of the IB program who would help underclassmen see IB as a prize, rather than a curse. They developed a network of seniors and returning graduates who would talk to new students about the program. The older students gave speeches—or sometimes wrote emails—that recalled how scared they had been of IB's reputation, and how they had found a way to get the work done despite their fears.

Crocker, Calhoon, Coast, and the counselors told freshmen and sophomores who were on the fence that they were not going to be trapped in IB. If it proved to be too much, they could switch to a more normal schedule. But it would be nearly impossible to move them up to IB from the regular courses after the beginning of the year, so why not keep their options open and sign up now?

The program was not cheap, and the Mount Vernon IB educators were happy that the school board picked up all the fees so that no student could cite cost as a reason for not enrolling in the courses. The school paid IB an annual subscription fee that by 2004 had reached $8,180, the same fee paid by every IB school in the United States. In addition, IB charged $142 over two years for every student seeking the full diploma and $79 for every junior or senior student seeking a certificate. There were also test registration fees of $73 for every diploma candidate and $51 for every certificate candidate. The IB received, in addition, $55 for every test taken and $35 for each extended essay submitted. In 2004 those student and test fees totalled $47,726, or a total Mount Vernon payment to IB of $55,906 for that year.

Fairfax County being more financially secure than many districts, there was also extra money from school headquarters to train IB teachers and pay a portion of the coordinator's salary. Some years Crocker even had enough to hold a two-week session in the summer for freshmen who were interested in seeing what the IB program might be like. She made sure minority students knew about the summer institute—she had one of the flyers done in Spanish—but it was open to all. Students were given a taste of a science lab, shown what it meant to be a critical thinker, and given other activities to reduce their fear of the unknown.

The flyer sent to parents for the July 2003 institute said: "Has your student thought about taking a Pre-IB or IB course? Is your student a bit uneasy about the workload? Has he or she heard that the classes are tough and there is even a summer assignment in some of the classes? If this sounds familiar, register your student for the IB Summer Institute to learn effective ways to approach homework, to meet the teachers, and to participate in a few mini-classes."

One of the secrets of expanding IB was working with the families. If a Mount Vernon IB educator had a conversation with a parent, she would ask if there were younger children who might also be interested. If a freshman or sophomore said he or she wanted to sign up for IB, the teacher would widen the invitation: "How about your three friends here? They can do it too." Students did not want to be in classes full of people they did not know, so signing up an entire group of friends made sense.

There would be lots of hard times during the year, Crocker knew. At some point in the spring when the exams loomed and the extended essays were due, at least one student—usually a senior—would decide to take a stand. Crocker had heard Calhoon deal with this more than once. The student would say, "I am not going to turn in that essay, Mrs. Calhoon. I have written it, but if I don't turn it in I can't earn the IB diploma."

"Come on, you can turn that in."

"Nope, I've made my decision. You can't make me earn the diploma."

And there were occasional moments in May when some students balked at taking an IB examination, although the Mount Vernon teachers had a number of ways to handle that.

"I'm not going to take that exam."

"Tell me why."

"Well, my college isn't going to give credit for it."

"No, that's not an acceptable answer. We need to know how good you are going to do against others. We need to know what you have learned. So you need to sit down for me and take that."

If the student still resisted, IB teachers would play their loyalty card. How could you do this to me? "These scores are going to come back here, you know, and show how well I have done, both in teaching you and making sure you take the exam. And you aren't going to take it?"

Sometimes even that didn't work. Brandon Hieskill, who graduated from Mount Vernon in 2001, said he liked the IB program and enjoyed all his teachers, particularly Cathy Scott in computer science, who remained a close advisor even after he went to college. But when he learned in January of his senior year that he had won a full scholarship to Washington and Lee University, he did not see any further need to get the full diploma. More specifically, he no longer wanted to endure the torture of trying to get his Spanish up to IB level. His college application success "clouded my judgment," he said, so he dropped out of Spanish. He passed all his other IB tests, he said, and found the experience helped greatly in college.

IB administrators and teachers at Mount Vernon expected that some seniors would blow off an exam or an essay. That was part of being a teenager. But they had to keep making their point, again and again and again, that hard work had its rewards. Not only did it take a while for the power of commitment to sink in with young people, but the school had a very high mobility rate, with students leaving and arriving all the time, so there was always someone who had not yet gotten the word.

Crocker, like many other IB school principals, did not like her faculty segregated, with some IB teachers and some non-IB teachers. She tried to make sure that all IB teachers taught regular courses, just as Dan Coast had taught ninth-grade biology as well as IB Biology. She thought teachers were better if they had a spectrum of students.

The IB tests were useful in revealing how teachers were doing. If Crocker saw a teacher's IB scores were higher than expected, she would celebrate the news and try to see how that teacher might be persuaded to share with others what she was doing. If the scores were lower than expected, Crocker would investigate the teacher's paperwork flow. That was often the thing that rookie instructors struggled with. There was so much to teach. The IB reading lists were so large. It was easy to fall behind and not return homework on time, or become buried in papers that had to be graded.

She asked those teachers many questions: What is your time frame? Is this paper necessary? Could you have asked for the same thing in three paragraphs rather than three pages? Are you working smart? Are you getting what you need? Are you getting too much of it? Is it worth reading all of that? What is your basic premise, and if you can get your basic premise in three sentences, why are you grading three full sheets?

After five years as principal, Crocker felt that the IB program had grown enough for people to be comfortable with it. She no longer had to explain to parents that IB meant International Baccalaureate. Whitman Middle School was raising the level of preparation by adopting the IB Middle Years Program. The number of people coming into Mount Vernon interested in pre-IB would be greater than ever.

She might have to stop herself in mid-sentence when she saw that a parent or child was puzzled with a term like "HL." She would explain that this meant Higher Level, a kind of IB course. But in the end, she learned, the labels did not matter nearly as much as the well-established confidence among parents that if their children came to Mount Vernon High School, they would get a quality education.

48

Starting Late, Finishing Strong

Breigh Miller heard about the International Baccalaureate program from her friend Deanna Pruitt. It was their freshman year at Mount Vernon High in 1999 and at first it sounded like too much work. Five years of a language and calculus too? She was just that year starting algebra and French, and she did not see how she could catch up.

IB had that effect on fourteen-year-olds who first encountered it. The five-hour exams, the 4,000-word essay, the community service requirements—they all seemed way too strange and way too painful. Even some teachers admitted they did not know much about it. Miller's parents were very accomplished in their careers—her father Ronald was in the army and her mother Janice was an office manager—but IB was new to them also.

College-level programs like IB and AP usually had few African American and Hispanic students. Education researchers had concluded years before that this was one reason why so many minority students seemed ill-prepared for college, and why only about 40 percent of minorities who started college eventually graduated, compared to 60 percent of non-Hispanic whites.

But Mount Vernon was different. By the time Miller graduated in 2003, about a third of IB students at the school, including her, were of African descent, matching the black percentage of the whole student body, something few other IB or AP schools ever managed to do. About 14 percent of IB students at Mount Vernon were Hispanic, compared to 19 percent of the total school enrollment. At Mount Vernon, unlike most U.S. public schools, students were welcomed into college-level courses the minute they expressed a wish to do so. There were no prerequisites, except for the math courses, and no other formal ways of deciding who would be admitted.

But like most schools, there were subtler, less formal screening devices, and one of them caught Miller early on. She had started school a few days late that year because her family had just moved to Fairfax County. The counselor she saw to set up her courses did not seem very interested in telling her much about IB and even less interested in getting her into the pre-IB classes. She was new to the area, had not been part of the preparatory courses at Whitman Middle School, and may have seemed to the counselor too much of a risk.

Her mother did not like the sound of that. She urged her daughter to go back and demand she be placed in the more challenging courses. But that was a hard thing for a new student who did not know much about the program. Her middle-school record was okay, but it included a couple of Cs. IB courses were tough. Rather than make a reputation for herself as a troublemaker, Miller decided that the counselor knew what was best.

As a result, she took no pre-IB courses in ninth grade. Next year, her counselor noticed she was getting no more Cs—a pledge Miller had made to herself—and he put her into a pre-IB English course with Stacia Zeimet. Miller loved that class and came close to getting all As that year, except for an annoying B-plus in geometry. Breigh rhymed with A, and that was what she was shooting for in each class.

IB courses were to start her junior year, but she was still not certain they were for her. Pruitt, her friend in the advanced orchestra class, described the pre-IB courses as rites of torture. The pre-IB algebra 2 and trigonometry course was particularly bad. "It is hard for us even to make a C," Pruitt said, somewhat frightening because if Miller decided to sign up for IB, that was exactly the math class she would have to take.

But Miller's good grades had given her confidence, and she went to see Calhoon. They sat down in the coordinator's office and looked at her grades so far. Calhoon pointed to the many As that year. "I think you would do well in IB, Breigh," she said.

Miller's father had just gotten his bachelor's degree in business administration at National Louis University and was starting on his master's degree despite his full-time military career. If he could do several things at the same time, Miller thought, she could too. So she signed up for IB, which turned out to be the greatest academic struggle of her life.

She had been getting As in regular courses without doing much work. The math had had its intricacies, forcing her to think hard occasionally, but she had an excellent memory. In most of those classes, if she did the reading, that was all she needed. No matter what she heard from Pruitt, she assumed she could breeze through IB classes as she had in her other courses. She was surprised when this assumption blew up in her face.

The counselor who didn't think she was ready for pre-IB in ninth grade, and put her in only one pre-IB course in tenth grade, had done her no favors. She was going in cold turkey, with little warning of what it was going to be like, and her new schedule was a killer. Her junior-year courses were French 111, IB Biology I, IB English 11, IB Social and Cultural Anthropology, pre-IB Government, pre-IB Algebra II/Trigonometry and IB History of the Americas. She should have had the two pre-IB courses the previous year, but she had to stuff them into an already full schedule.

Calhoon gave her the usual warning about overextending herself outside the classroom. Miller decided to drop advanced orchestra. It was often the high point of her day in the early high school years, and she would miss it, but there was no longer enough time for it.

The first marking period hit her hard. For the first time in high school she did not make the honor roll, not even the lower-level honors list that allowed you to get a C-plus. The C that had ruined it was in math. She had thought of herself as a decent math student. It was one of her weaker subjects, the opposite of her great strength, writing, but she had been getting Bs until she encountered Teresa Thaxton, who raised the bar so much Miller wondered if she could ever jump that high.

Thaxton was a nice lady, Miller thought, but not a nice math teacher. She had very neat handwriting on the board, which Miller appreciated, but when she started to speak, telling them precisely what they were in for, the classroom became very quiet. Grading was hard. Fear was in the air. The only sign of relief came at the Thanksgiving break when Thaxton offered the first opportunity for her students to earn extra credit, usually a common practice in American high school courses.

To soothe her bruised brain after math class, Miller slid into the warm bubbling bath of literature that was Emmet Rosenfeld's IB English 11 class. Miller thought he was one of the brightest and coolest teachers she had ever had, in part because he let the students run the class. He explained how the course would work and how it would be carried on into the senior year. He left it up to the students to make sure they met the requirements and deadlines, as if they were already in college.

They organized themselves into study groups of three or four students each. In Miller's group were Vivian Obando, Tyeesha Johnson, and Danielle Miller, no relation. She began to think of them as "my girls." The English class lessons took on a life they would not otherwise have had without the jokes and debates among the group over what they were reading.

Miller particularly liked "spinning plates," Rosenfeld's way of having different groups read different books but discuss the devices and themes they were seeing together. It was clear to Rosenfeld that Miller was particularly adept at such analysis, and was becoming the backbone of her group. She was businesslike, earnest, and dependable. She did a fine job with her PowerPoint presentation on Zora Hurston, but was distressed when Rosenfeld gave her only a B-plus because of too many spelling and grammar mistakes. She insisted on identifying all the flaws and resubmitting the work.

Her group was a hit at April-fest, a class-organized carnival that reflected themes in their reading. Tyeesha Johnson, who struggled in the class because of her responsibilities as a teenage mother, poured enormous effort into an elaborate poster for the festival. Miller appeared in a camouflage costume and made sure she participated in all of her classmate's games.

Miller also had fun in Allen Rushing's History of the Americas course. Rushing gave longer reading assignments and more writing assignments than her other teachers, but she never felt like they were a burden.

All in all, IB was a pain. But Miller stuck with it. The Anthropology course was her elective, and she would later consider it one of her most fortunate choices. Pruitt had spoken well of it, and the more Miller got into it, the more she loved its exploration of cultures she knew nothing about. It helped explain differences that she had long noticed, and wondered about. Her paper in that course was so good it was selected as a model for other IB schools to study.

Yet, despite the occasional good day, Miller was still getting less than acceptable grades, at least by her standards. For a while she wondered if college was going to be something she would really want to do. The crisis of confidence was common in young people who would be the first in their family to go right to college after high school. For a while the extraordinary demands of IB made her feel less confident than she would have been if she had been taking a standard college prep program, and getting As for modest work. She did not appreciate how unusual a course IB was. She thought that if she was struggling in high school, how could she handle the workload of a college student? She thought, wrongly, that college would be significantly harder than IB.

She survived eleventh grade, just barely, and as her senior year started she began to feel a little better. She did not have to take so many extra courses, except for physics and biology at the same time because physics was required for the IB diploma. She began applying to colleges and heard admiring statements from recruiters about her courage and good sense at being in IB. She began to tell herself the same story. "I'm taking the most challenging course offered to high school students around the world," she said. "And even though I have had some tough times, it will work out for the best when I get to college."

Her English 12 course in international literature with Kimberly Reakes was often as stimulating as junior English had been with Rosenfeld. But she still faced the 4,000-word extended essay. Just the thought of writing that much—at least fifteen typewritten pages—was exhausting. Several seniors dropped out of the diploma program because they could not handle the project. They would get full credit for their IB courses, but they could not receive the full IB diploma without writing the paper.

The topic Miller selected was the women artists, writers, and performers of the Harlem Renaissance of the 1920s and 1930s. She decided to investigate how their successes influenced prominent women in their work today. The female artists and writers in Harlem had been part of a continuum of women that went back centuries, but it was a rare moment in history for African American women to gain so much respect in so many cultural pursuits, Miller thought.

The Harlem Renaissance, she discovered, was a time of enhancement and enlightenment within black culture. All the women in her paper, such as Hurston, had significant impact on many of the female writers that followed, both black and white.

When she turned the paper in to Calhoon in December, it felt like a great weight had been taken off her back. She had finished it by the due date, and the deadlines she knew she would have in college seemed less frightening.

She got her IB diploma and enrolled at Georgia State University in Atlanta. She found the workload manageable. Study habits developed in IB prepared her well for the college routine. She felt she was able to contribute her ideas in class and fulfill her highest expectations. It began to occur to her that IB was not just about college, but about getting ready for life.

Taking seven extremely demanding courses in her junior year of high school was a terrible risk. In a way, the counselor who kept her out of pre-IB had been right. She had not been nearly as well prepared to take on the load as she should have been. But it was the struggle that made her strong, and she was happy to have had a chance to measure herself against a tough, incorruptible standard. Asked during her first year in college how she felt, she thought for a moment, and then typed out an email summing it all up: "I feel good now knowing that I achieved the IB Diploma and that it was well earned."

Index

DATE DUE